THE CORPORATE CREDIT BIBLE:

The How-to Guide to Running your Corporation or LLC

ROBERT K BOSCARATO

ISBN-13:
978-1495471537

ISBN-10:
1495471535

:

DEDICATION

This Book is for my fans and friends I hope it brings you money and happiness to build a business the brings the good life to you

ACKNOWLEDGMENTS

The Author Gratefully thanks Mr. and Mrs. Matt C Skaggs for the
book career idea and all the time they put into the book themes

Try selling your business

Know when to fold'em if you owe $20.00 more
then you have you should file bankrupt get out of
business

Table of Contents

Chapter 1: The Corporate Structure & Basic Terminology

Congratulations! The decision to incorporate your business is the first step in providing effective protection from personal liability, excessive taxation, and provides the entrepreneur or the savvy investor with an effective and powerful tool to aid in managing and growing your business ventures. There are many reasons to incorporate; by incorporating, you are forming a separate, distinct legal entity that can be utilized to safeguard your personal wealth and assets by separating you, personally, from business liability, lawsuits, creditors and excessive taxation.

By forming a Corporation or LLC, you are forming a separate "person", a legal entity that can own property, pay taxes, enter contracts and create income that is separate from yours. A corporation can sue and be sued on its own, thereby safeguarding the personal assets of the shareholders. This separation and safeguarding of personal assets and property is known as "limited liability." Other advantages include perpetuity of the business, as the business is not affected by the changing of the shareholders due to death, transfer of shares, sales, acquisitions, etc.

Another key advantage is that potential vendors, creditors, partners as well as investors in your business associate the "inc." after your company's name as an indication that they are dealing with a company that is viable and professionally run. Further, savvy investors will recognize the increased protection from personal liability and undue taxation that an incorporated business provides.

The Corporate Ladder

The Rung at the Top of the Ladder

The Board of Directors is the governing body of the corporation that directs the fundamental policies and major undertakings of the corporation. The directors usually elect the president and leave general operations and day-to-day business to the president and other officers under their employ, but usually require consulting before any substantive decisions or agreements are entered into.

Members of the Board of Directors can also be officers, but this is not mandatory or necessarily so--the titles can be whatever the shareholders want them to be, though these must generally be outlined in the bylaws of the corporation. Further, many times positions can be combined with one person holding more than one title, and with various positions holding different reporting obligations (for example, in some cases, the President may be asked to report to the CEO, while in other organizations, the CEO may be asked to report to the President). Or they can even have multiple people holding the same title (which is often the case with the Vice President title).

The Corporate Shareholders

Shareholders (also called stockholders) are the owners of a corporation. As such, the board of directors and the officers of the company owe a fiduciary duty to the shareholders to do what is in their best interest as a group. Specific shareholder rights are outlined in company bylaws and in state law, and these laws vary from state to state. Though specific duties and reporting practices vary from state to state, the shareholders generally vote on the president, the election of the board of directors and any major changes in the composition or organization of the corporation.

A shareholder or stockholder in a corporation can be an individual or another company or corporation that is considered an "owner" of the existing corporation because it legally owns at least one share in the stock of the corporation. Usually holding the right to one vote per share on matters such as elections to the board of directors, the right to share in distributions of the company's income, the right to purchase new shares issued by the company, and the right to a company's assets during a liquidation of the company, the person or persons who own a majority of the stock can generally vote in the board that best suits their interests and run the company.

Another important point to note is that although directors and officers of a company are bound by fiduciary duties to act in the best interest of the shareholders, the shareholders themselves normally do not have such duties towards each other.

Corporate Officers

A Corporate Officer is a high ranking

person in a given corporation that is assigned a title indicating his position within the corporation. While a corporation may have many positions under its purview, only the persons holding the highest ranking positions are considered "corporate officers" (or executives). Corporate officers typically consist of the President, Vice president, treasurer and secretary. A corporation can choose to have more officer positions, but these are the standard, best practices positions. Many states allow one person to hold all of the offices, but this may not be the best practices approach. The authority and responsibilities of each officer are outlined in the corporate bylaws.

Most Corporations' Officers

include but are not limited to the following positions:

- Chief Executive Officer (CEO)
  - President
  - Secretary
  - Treasurer
- Chief Financial Officer (CFO)
- Chief Operating Officer (COO)
- Chief Information Officer (CIO) and (Fractional CIO)
  - Chief Information Security Officer (CISO)
- Chief Knowledge Officer (CKO)
  - Vice President
  - Director-General
  - Managing Director
  - Executive Director

The President

The President of the corporation is

usually elected by the Board of Directors and is responsible for carrying out the orders issued by the Board of Directors. The President is the figure head of the corporation.

The Secretary

The Secretary plays a vital role in that he or she is responsible for the upkeep and safeguarding of corporate records. This includes, but is not limited to, the formation documents, the corporate minutes, and any business transactions or written agreements entered into or on behalf of the corporation.

The Treasurer

The Treasurer is responsible for the

management of all corporate funds, bank accounts, lines of credit, and for recording all corporate financial transactions. While many of these duties are self-directed, the Treasurer takes his or her direction from the Board of Directors.

Corporate Resolutions

Corporate resolutions are written resolutions that serve to outline strategy, compensation, and benefits to the shareholders and officers of a corporation. While they are not required for every corporate decision, it is a best practice procedure to record the major decisions of the corporation in the form of written resolutions. This strengthens the corporation's legal shield by providing solid evidence that any actions were taken on behalf of the corporation and not on behalf of the owners or officers.

Corporate Bylaws

Corporate bylaws, or the "rules" for the corporation and its shareholders, are drafted by a corporation's founders or directors under the authority of its Charter or Articles of Incorporation. Bylaws widely vary from organization to organization, but generally cover topics such as how directors are elected, how meetings of directors and shareholders are conducted, and what officers the organization will have and a description of their duties. They can generally be amended by an organization's Board of Directors

We cannot stress highly enough that failure to observe and implement any of these formalities will serve to diminish and mitigate the protections offered by the formation of the Corporation and will allow outside entities (the IRS, creditors, claimants/plaintiffs, potential adverse litigants, etc.) to "pierce the corporate veil" and peer into the inner workings and assets of the Corporation, it's Officers, Directors and Shareholders. This will be explained in further detail.

Information Frequently Required on Incorporation Documents

If you are considering forming your business as a corporation, one question you may have is, "what information is required on the incorporation documents?" Knowing this ahead of time helps you save time as you begin the incorporation process.

The formation document for a corporation is called the articles of incorporation or certificate of incorporation. Each state has its own version of this document creating a number of variances in the amount and type of information required.

Company Name: The desired name of the corporation must be included. That name must typically contain a corporate identifier, such as "Corporation," "Incorporated," "Company," or an abbreviation of those terms, such as "Inc."

Undertaking a preliminary name availability search prior to submitting the articles of incorporation will help to see if your desired name is available. Keep in mind that the state holds final approval rights on the desired name to ensure it is not already in use by another company in that state or is not "deceptively similar" to a name already in use.

Business Purpose: The business purpose is an explanation of what the company is formed to do or provide.

There are two types of business purpose clauses: general and specific.

General business purpose – some states will accept a general-purpose clause, which basically states that the company is formed to engage in "all lawful business."

Specific business purpose – some states require a more complete explanation of the types of products and/or services the company will provide. Registered Agent: Virtually all states require corporations to have a <u>registered agent</u> in the state of formation. The registered agent is the party responsible for the receipt of important legal and tax documents for the corporation. The registered agent must have a physical address (no P.O. boxes) in the state of formation and must be available during normal business hours. Examples of documents sent to the registered agent include Service of Process (or notice of litigation), which is the document that initiates a lawsuit; mail from the state; and often taxation documentation from the state's department of taxation. One thing to note is the registered agent address is a matter of public record. In states that do not require the legal address of the business to be included in the formation documents, the registered agent address is the only address on file for the company. Many business owners, particularly home-based businesses, choose to use a registered agent provider both to ensure these important documents are professionally handled and to keep their addresses out of the hands of marketers.

Incorporator: The incorporator is the person or company preparing and filing the formation documents with the state. Most states require the name and signature of the incorporator to be included in the formation documents and some also require the incorporator's address be included.

Number of Authorized Shares of Stock: Corporations must outline the number of shares of stock they wish to authorize. While many people think only public companies have shares of stock, the reality is that all corporations, no matter how small, have stock. Stock represents the ownership in a corporation. As you consider how many shares of stock to authorize, keep in mind that a corporation does not need to issue the total number of authorized shares. Some corporations opt to hold a certain number of un-issued shares in order to add additional owners at a later date or to increase the ownership percentage for a current shareholder.

Share Par Value: The par value of a share is its minimum stated value.

Par value typically doesn't correlate to the actual value of a share. Common par values are $0.01, $1.00 or no par. The actual value of a share is its fair market value, or what someone is willing to pay for a share of stock. For public companies, actual value is determined by the price investors are willing to pay for each share on a national exchange. For private companies, the actual value of a share is typically determined by the overall value of the corporation or the book value.

Preferred Shares: If a corporation plans to authorize both common and preferred shares, this information along with any information on voting rights must be included in the articles of incorporation. Preferred shares typically provide those shareholders with preferential payments of dividends or distribution of assets should the company cease operations. Many small business owners choose to only authorize shares of common stock. For additional information on preferred shares and voting rights it is best to seek the advice of an attorney. Directors: Many states require the names and addresses of the initial directors of the corporation to be included on the formation documents. The directors are the individuals responsible for overseeing and directing the affairs of the corporation, including making major corporate decisions. They are not responsible for the day-to-day activities of the business, which are the responsibility of a corporation's officers. Directors are elected by the shareholders and are also responsible for appointing the officers.

Officers: While inclusion of the officer information is optional in many states, a few states do require it. The officers are responsible for the day-to-day activities of the corporation. Common officer titles include president, vice president, secretary and treasurer.

Legal Address of the Company: Supplying the legal address, or the principal address, of the business is optional in many states but a few states do require it.

While this is not a complete list of everything a state might require on its articles of incorporation, it outlines the typical items and will help you assemble this information prior to starting the incorporation process.

Registered Agent: What You Need to Know

As you prepare to form your business as a corporation or limited liability company (LLC), you need to select a registered agent. Virtually all states require corporations and LLC's that are formed or foreign qualified (registered to transact business) there to have a registered agent in that state; however, many business owners have no idea what a registered agent is or does.

The registered agent is responsible for receiving important legal and tax documents on behalf of the business. Types of documents sent to the registered agent include Service of Process (sometimes called notice of litigation), which is the document that initiates a lawsuit; important mail sent by the state, such as annual reports or statements; and tax documents sent by the state's department of taxation.

The registered agent must have a physical address in the state of formation or qualification. Post Office boxes or a private mailbox rented from a company, such as the UPS Store, are not allowed. The registered agent must also be available during normal business hours. Additionally, the registered agent's address is a matter of public record, which means that anyone has access to it. In states that do not require a company's legal address be included in the formation or qualification documents, the registered agent's address is the only address on file with the state for that company.

Individuals are allowed to act as registered agent for a business. For example, if you have a physical address in the state where you for your corporation or LLC, you could name yourself as the agent. You could not, however, name your new company as its own registered agent. In order for a company to act as a registered agent, it must typically be approved to do so by the state in question.

There are companies, such as American Corporate Credit, that provide registered agent services to other businesses for an annual fee.

You may be saying, "I'm a one-person company, why should I use a registered agent provider?" In reality, these companies provide a lot of value to even to the smallest of businesses, such as providing online access to Service of Process and providing tools to assist with the ongoing compliance requirements corporations and LLC's face.

As you are evaluating who should be the registered agent for your business, below are some items to keep in mind and some situations for which using a registered agent service provider may be the best choice for your business.

- You're forming your company in a state where you don't have a physical location. You are legally required to have a registered agent with a physical address (no P.O. Box) in the state of formation. Using a professional registered agent provider helps you satisfy this requirement.

- You use a Post Office box as your business address. You cannot act as the registered agent for your business if you have only a P.O. Box or a private mailbox as your only address.
- Your company does business in several states. When you qualify your company to transact business in states other than your state of formation, you need a registered agent in each of those states. By using a registered agent service provider, one company is handling this important documentation for you in each state and allowing you to concentrate on your business.
- Your address changes frequently. It is important to keep the registered agent address updated

with the state, but changing it requires a formal state filing and may also require that a fee be paid to the state. If you name yourself as agent, you will be responsible for undertaking this process to keep your address current. By using a registered agent service provider, you never have to worry about this.

- Your business is home-based. As previously mentioned, the registered agent address is a matter of public record. That means anyone, including marketers, can access it. It is not uncommon for the registered agent to receive a lot of "junk mail" for the business. Using a registered agent provider can reduce the amount of unsolicited mail your business receives.

- You prefer to keep business activities private. When a company receives a Service of Process, this document is often delivered by local law enforcement. Most business owners do not want the sheriff to show up in front of customers, employees or neighbors (as in the case of home-based businesses) serve them notice that their company is being sued. Using a professional registered agent ensures you receive any Service of Process discreetly.

- You don't maintain normal business hours. The registered agent for a business must be available during normal business hours to accept important documents as they are delivered. If you set your own hours, you may wish to consider using a professional provider, so that you never miss these important communications.

- You do not have a permanent worksite. If your business requires you to move around frequently, for example an electrician who is making service calls all day, using a registered agent service provider ensures that important documents will still reach you and your business.
- You want one less thing to worry about. Running your company is challenging enough without personally handling the necessary minutia. A professional registered agent can often help you by

providing online access to your accounts and important documents and assisting with the annual filings states impose on corporations and LLC's. Service of Process has been mentioned frequently in this section and for good reason. It is very important that this document be handled properly and promptly. As previously mentioned, a Service of Process initiates a lawsuit against your company. The Service of Process also typically outlines the timeframe in which a response from your company must be received. If a response is not received in time, a default judgment may be issued. When a default judgment is issued, the other party wins, and your company may need to pay the damages outlined.

As you form or foreign qualify your corporation or LLC, give some additional thought to who will be the registered agent for your company. While the registered agent is a legal requirement, the right registered agent can also be an asset to your business.

Chapter 2: Types of Corporations

There are a number of benefits afforded by forming your business as a corporation; chief among these benefits are the protections from personal liability and asset seizure that are offered to the owners/shareholders of a corporation. These protections limit the legal and business liabilities (protection from lawsuits and debts) encountered by the corporation because it is treated as a separate, legal entity. There are also favorable taxation, deductible employee benefits, personal asset protection, anonymity, ease of raising capital, and credibility benefits that are the hallmark of an incorporated business.

Other beneficial features of a corporation are its broad range of powers and flexibility beyond that of a sole proprietorship --a corporation can have its own bank accounts, own property, conduct business, and even establish a line of credit, irrespective of the individual accounts or credit of the shareholders. It can sue and be sued, hire staff, and engage in business dealings, all the while maintaining itself as an entity separate from its shareholders. Just as you or I need to file our own taxes, a corporation must do the same. Keep in mind that different types of corporations are better suited with different types of business. It is not a "one size fits all" solution, therefore different types of corporations offer different advantages, and disadvantages.

You can incorporate your business without an attorney. However, it is critical that certain, specific wording is included in the articles of incorporation, by-laws, minutes for meetings and other documents so that the corporation can provide legal protection, tax savings and other important corporate benefits. Professionally prepared articles of incorporation, by-laws and minutes are provided in certain American Corporate Credit Services packages, or a la carte.

After the initial requirements are met (the person forming the corporation must be a U.S. resident, and in some states, a U.S. Citizen, of legal age, and that person must provide their name and physical address), it all starts by choosing a name for your new corporation, and a back-up name. The back-up name (your second choice) is necessary in the event that your first choice is not available. Additional person's names can be added to the corporation after it has been filed. Once that is done, it is time to elect the state in which you wish to incorporate. There are many things to consider when it comes to picking a state, with things like management versus shareholder rights, franchise tax, etc. playing important decision-making roles. Once done, American Corporate Credit Services then conducts a search with the Secretary of State in the state that you have elected in order to ensure that your name is available, and if the search comes up with no conflicts, your name is reserved. Then we take it from there, conducting the filings, assigning a registered agent, etc., with you only needing to provide the necessary fees to cover the set-up and filing costs, and thereafter observing the corporate formalities.

C Corporation

A traditional Corporation (or a "C" Corporation) is a business structure that is created as a separate, distinct legal entity from its owners (or "shareholders"). Once a corporation is formed, the corporation can have its own bank accounts, own property, conduct business, and even establish a line of credit, irrespective of the individual accounts or credit of the shareholders. The primary advantage to having a business formed as a corporation is the fact that the shareholders are not personally liable for the debts and legal liabilities incurred by the corporation. For example, if a corporation is sued for business reasons and loses, the shareholders will not be required to satisfy the debts of the corporation from their own personal assets. This safeguards assets and properties of the individual shareholders, and as such, is more attractive to potential investors.

Once a corporation is established, the shareholders must name (via election) a board of directors that is responsible for the operation of the business, making business decisions, and managing all business-related affairs. This board is elected by the shareholders of the corporation, and once named; the board appoints "officers" of the corporation to specific duties. This usually includes a secretary, a treasurer, etc.

Another important thing to know about the formation and maintenance of a corporation is that certain corporate formalities must be observed. These are things like a required annual meeting of the board of directors, the necessity to maintain the corporate "minutes," the separation of corporate and personal funds (no "co-mingling" of funds), and a necessity to maintain written agreements for all corporate transactions (including internal transactions such as internal loans, executive compensation agreements, etc.).

Advantages of a C Corporation

- Limited Liability for Shareholders
- Tax Savings
- Easy Transfer of ownership
- Privacy

- Asset Protection
- Prestige for the Business and Corporate Officers
- Credibility
- Centralized Management
- Ability to raise capital and attract investors

A major disadvantage of the traditional corporation is the dreaded "double taxation" dilemma. A traditional C Corporation pays tax on all corporate (business) income, and then once a distribution is made to the shareholders, the individual shareholders pay income tax again on these distributions (or dividends). One way to avoid the double taxation dilemma is to establish the corporation as a "pass through" entity like a partnership wherein all corporate profits pass through to the individual shareholders and they are then responsible for the tax burden.

A corporation that has made the election to be treated in this manner (by making the appropriate filings and meeting the requirements) is known as an "S Corporation."

Disadvantages of a C Corporation

- Double Taxation pitfall
- Increased paperwork
- Necessity of exercising the corporate formalities

Incorporating is one of the first legal steps towards taking your business venture to the next level and important if raising capital is necessity. A Savvy investor would review business model and position, and see the "inc." after your business as a sign that the business is a serious venture and worthy of his investment. This is a critical step towards making investors feel comfortable and give serious consideration towards investing capital in your enterprise!

<u>S Corporation</u>

All Corporations start out as a regular Corporation. By filing form 2553 with the IRS you are electing to meet the requirements for an S-Corporation. An S Corporation (named in such a manner because of its organization meeting the IRS requirements to be taxed under Subchapter S of the Internal Revenue Code) is a corporation that is structured in such a manner as to provide a pass-through entity for tax purposes, much like a partnership whose income or losses "pass through" to the individual shareholders' personal tax returns (in direct proportion to their investment or ownership in the company), while still providing the same protections for assets and from liabilities as a traditional corporation. The shareholders will pay personal income taxes based on the S corporation's income, regardless of whether or not the income is actually distributed, but they will avoid the "double taxation" that is inherent to the traditional corporation (or "C" corporation).

The Major Difference between C Corporations and S Corporations

Because of its "pass through" taxation structure, the S corporation is not subject to taxes at the corporate level, and hence avoids the pitfalls of "double taxation" (in a standard or traditional corporation, business income is first taxed at the corporate level, then the distribution of the residual income to the individual shareholders is taxed again as personal "income") that befalls C corporations.

Unlike C corporation dividends which are taxed at the federal rate of 15.00%, S corporation dividends (or more properly titled "Distributions") are taxed at the shareholder's marginal tax rate. However, the c corporation dividend is subject to the double-taxation mentioned above. The income is first taxed at the corporate level before it is distributed as a dividend and then taxed as income when issued to the individual shareholders.

For example, Cogs Inc, is formed as an S corporation, makes $20 million in net income and is owned 51% by Jack and 49% by Tom. On Jack's personal tax return, he will report $10.2 million in income and Tom will report $9.8 million. If Jack (as the majority owner) decides not to distribute the net income profit, both Jack and Tom will still be liable for taxes on the earnings as if a distribution was made in that manner, even though neither received any cash distribution. This is an example of a corporate "squeeze-play" that can be used in an attempt to force out a minority partner.

Business Goals of an S Corporation

Having S corporation status provides for a few substantial benefits for a corporation. First and foremost, of course, is the goal of achieving limited liability, or mitigating the impact of personal law suits, or other forms of debt incurred by individual shareholders, against shareholders, and protecting against them impacting the corporation as a whole, or the rest of the shareholders as individuals. This asset protection benefit is true of both the traditional corporation and the S corporation. More specific to the selection of an S corporation is the pass-through taxation benefit. While there are limitations as to the amount of shareholders that a corporation can have in order to meet the IRS requirements for S corporation status, most corporations that fit the size threshold (in most cases, not more than 75 to 100 shareholders) elect to be taxed as an S corporation because it allows the individual shareholders to earn a larger distribution of the business income. The corporation can pass income directly to shareholders and avoid the double taxation that is inherent with the dividends of public companies, while still enjoying the advantages of the corporate structure.

Electing S Corporation Status

Electing S corporation status has tax liability implications. S status allows shareholders to apply company profits and losses to individual income tax returns. In order to elect S status, one must first incorporate as a general C corporation and then file IRS form 2553. If you have recently incorporated, your corporation may file for S status anytime during the tax year within 75 days of your incorporation date. Otherwise, this action must be taken by March 15 if the corporation is a calendar year taxpayer, in order for the election to take effect for the current tax year. A corporation may later decide to elect S corporation status, but this decision would not take effect until the following year.

Passive Income Caution

Passive income is any income generated by an investment; i.e. stocks, bonds, equity-type investments, real estate, etc. Active income is generated by services rendered, products sold, etc. It is important to make sure that your S corporation's passive income does not exceed 25% of the corporation's gross receipts over a consecutive three year period; otherwise your corporation would be in danger of having its S status revoked by the IRS. A better choice if your business is expected to have substantial passive income may be an LLC.

Qualifying for S Corporation Status

In order to qualify for S corporation status a few requisite measures must be met:

1. The corporation must be formed as a general, for-profit C class corporation.
2. be sure that your corporation has only issued one class of stock.
3. All the shareholders are U.S. Citizens or Permanent Residents.
4. There can be no more than 75 shareholders.
5. Your corporation's passive income level does not pass the 25% of gross receipts limit.
6. If your corporation has a tax-year

end date other than December 31, you must file for permission from the IRS. If your corporation has met all the above, you may file form 2553 with the IRS to elect S status.

S Corporation vs. LLC

A Limited Liability Company can be owned (have as "members") corporations, other LLC's, partnerships, trusts and non-US citizen, non-resident aliens. The S corporation, on the other hand, can only be owned by individual US citizens or permanent resident aliens. An LLC may offer different levels/classes of membership while an S corporation may only offer one class of stock. An LLC may have any number of members but an S corporation is limited to a maximum of 75 to 100 shareholders (depending on the rules of the state in which it is formed). When a shareholder of an S corporation is sued in a personal (not a business) lawsuit, the shares of stock are an asset that may be seized. When a member of an LLC is sued in a personal (not a business) lawsuit, there are provisions to protect the membership stake from being taken from the individual.

Legal Issues to Consider with an S Corporation

To be sure, there are certain regulatory steps and requirements that need to be met before a corporation can be treated as an S corporation. First, the shareholders of an existing corporation (or the originator of a new corporation) must make an election to be an S corporation on IRS Form 2553 (and the corresponding form for the state in which the corporation was incorporated) before the 16th day of the third month following the close of the C corporation tax year if the election is to be effective for the current tax year. The C Corporation must qualify as an eligible corporation during those 2 1/2 months and all shareholders during those 2 1/2 months must consent, even if they do not own stock at the time of the election. If the election is filed after the 15th day of the third month of the tax year, the election will be in effect for the next tax year and all shareholders at the time of the election must consent.

Termination of S Corporation Status

Voluntary termination of an S election is made by filing a statement with the Service Center where the original election was properly filed. A revocation may be made only with the consent of shareholders who, at the time the revocation is made, hold more than one-half of the number of issued and outstanding shares of stock (including nonvoting stock) of the corporation. There is specific information that must be included in the statement and this information is outlined in Regulations section 1.1362-6(a) (3) and in Instructions for IRS Form 1120S, U.S. Income Tax

Return for an S Corporation

The revocation may state an effective date as long as it is on or after the date the revocation is filed. If no date is specified and the revocation is filed before the 15th day of the third month of the tax year, the revocation will be effective for the current tax year. If the revocation is filed after the 15th day of the third month of the tax year, the revocation will be effective for the next tax year. .

Should I Organize My Enterprise as an S Corporation?

If you intend for your corporation to have more than a few shareholders (but less than the limit in your individual state) and you can appreciate the benefits of pass-through taxation while at the same time understanding the potential pitfalls involved with the "taxation irrespective of distribution," and you meet the legal requirements outlined above, then the S corporation can go a long way towards making your business profitable and attractive to the right investors!

Professional Corporation

Groups of certain professionals can form corporations known as professional corporations or professional service corporations ("PC"). The list of professionals covered by professional corporation status differs from state to state;

though it typically covers accountants, engineers, physicians and other health care professionals, lawyers, psychologists, social workers, and veterinarians. Typically, these professionals must be organized for the sole purpose of providing a professional service (for example, a law corporation must be made up of licensed attorneys). A professional corporation offers many of the limited liability and taxation benefits offered by a C corporation.

In certain states, this is the only incorporation option available for certain professionals, whereas in others, they are given the choice of being either a professional corporation or S or C corporation. Professional corporations can shield owners from liability. While it can't protect a professional from his/her own malpractice liability, it can protect against liability from negligence of an associate and this is the primary reason professional's form these type of corporations.

Non-Profit Corporations

Non-profit Corporations are formed in order to conduct activities and transactions for purposes other than shareholder financial gain, while at the same time providing the same asset protections and limited liabilities of a standard corporation. A non-profit corporation can make a profit, but this profit must be used strictly to forward the goals rather than to provide earned income (in the form of dividends) to its shareholders. It is understood that most of the transactions and activities of a Non-profit corporation will not be commercial in nature.

The Major Difference between Non-Profit and For-Profit Organizations

Most experts consider that it is the legal and ethical restrictions on the distribution of profits to owners or shareholders which fundamentally distinguishes nonprofits from "for-profit", or commercial enterprises. A more precise term to describe most non-profit organizations is 'not-for-profit', rather than 'non-profit', and this is often used in legislation and texts.

Non-profit corporations generally do not operate to generate profit, a defining characteristic of such organizations. However, a nonprofit organization may accept, hold and disburse money and other things of value, and it may also legally and ethically trade at a profit, provided that the proviso that any profit generated will be used to further its cause, goal or mission is adhered to. The extent to which it can generate income may be constrained, or the use of those profits may be restricted. Nonprofits therefore are typically funded by donations from the private or public sector, and often have tax exempt status. Private donations may sometimes be tax deductible.

*Additionally, a nonprofit organization may have members as opposed to shareholders.

Chapter 3: LLC Basics

A limited liability company, or LLC, is a form of business organization that allows for limited liability for an unlimited number of shareholders that they might not have otherwise enjoyed had they formed as a simple partnership, but all the while maintaining most of the taxation benefits afforded by a partnership. Because of these dual benefits, the shareholders, or "Members" as they are known if part of an LLC, basically enjoy the same types of limited liability protection that a corporation offers, with very few exceptions, and at the same time, also enjoy certain tax advantages, including, but not limited to, pass-through taxation and partnership treatment by the IRS. These advantages make LLC's very desirable for certain business dealings and ventures.

After limiting individual member liability and thus providing for the protection of member assets, the advantage of "pass through taxation" can be one of the key benefits offered by an LLC. The profits or losses of the business, whether or not there is an actual distribution, pass directly through to the Member's personal income tax return (IRS Form 1040) and by-pass the typical "business profit" tax at the company level. The LLC files a Form 1065, and then lists each member's taxable profit on IRS Form K-1. This pass through taxation is one of the hallmarks of the tax advantages available to an LLC. Because of this tax treatment, the LLC is not subject to the double taxation pitfall that befalls standard corporations (where income is taxed at the corporate or company level as profit, then again at the individual shareholder level as earned income).

The net profit of the LLC is not considered to be income earned by the Members, though portions distributed to the Managing Member (if the LLC is thusly structured) can be treated as such via the "fringe benefit" treatment called for by the IRS.

Advantages of the LLC form of business organization

- An LLC allows members, like shareholders in a corporation, to enjoy limited liability. The LLC is a separate, legal entity and thus its assets are considered separate and apart from Member's assets save for the amount invested by the member in the LLC.

- An LLC, if properly organized, enjoys the advantage of pass-through taxation, whereby business profit is treated as having "passed through" the entity and onto the individual members, via the 1065 form filed by the LLC, and thus avoiding tax at the corporate level, and again at the member level ("double taxation").

- Corporations are allowed as members of an LLC. This further level of tiered ownership increases the limited liability aspect of an LLC, and makes for greater features and benefit options for the owner.
- Less strict organizational rules and an absence of the "corporate formalities." Depending on how it is structured, an LLC can be completely driven (managed) by the operating agreement, with no special need for annual meetings or special notations or record keeping.
- Unlike an S Corporation, there is no limit to the number of members allowed by an LLC.

Some of the disadvantages of an LLC are

- Because of the pass-through profit designation via the 1065 form, all income "distributed" to the individual members' K1s is treated as member income, irrespective of any actual distributions. This highlights a situation potentially controlled by the managing member, and is one of the "powers" that may need to be addressed via the operating agreement.
- When a corporation is a member of an LLC, the owner of the corporation can be subject to taxation from the LLC's income.
- There is no perpetuity with an LLC, with its term usually specifically outlined.

LLC Formation

The process of forming an LLC is

very similar to that of incorporating, with the notable exception that the documents filed with the state are known as the Articles of Organization and the company owners are known as LLC members (versus "shareholders"). The rules are a bit different state by state, of course, but the formation is basically the same.

The formation begins with the filing of the appropriate documents with the appropriate state agency. Once your LLC is filed, you should create and then adopt an operating agreement that is used to govern your company. The operating agreement is a legal document wherein the management type, ownership and interest, allocation of power and many other forms of company operations are described in legal detail. The operating agreement is not generally filed or recorded with any state or federal office, but it is a best practice, due-diligence requirement for any well-organized LLC. Most states accept single member LLC's, though some specify at least two members. Please note that there can be tax consequences associated with a single member LLC, and thus it may be more prudent to form as a corporation instead in some instances. That is definitely an option that should be considered.

Some LLC's are managed by its members, or in the alternative, you may elect to assign managers to the LLC, similar in nature to corporate officers. When an LLC is run by managers, their power and control should be, and most often times is, managed explicitly by provisions outlined in the operating agreement. Other important things that should be properly and thoroughly outlined in the operating agreement include voting rights, distribution of interest, distribution of profits, etc. The management structure can be arranged so that the manager has 100% control and little to no ownership. This may be an ideal arrangement to maximize asset protection.

There are other benefits to forming as an LLC rather than a corporation. For example, while a an S corporation may allow for many of the same liability protections and asset distribution benefits of an LLC, it is limited to between 75 and 100 shareholders, and none of these shareholders can be in the form of a Corporation or IRA's (in direct contrast to an LLC which does permit corporations as member). These rules limit the subchapter "S" option to smaller organizations or forcing the buyback or buyout of stockholders for those organizations wishing to convert to an S corporation. Additionally, there are ventures of limited duration, such as movie production, or the collaboration on a limited real estate venture, where the perpetuity of a corporation is neither necessary, nor prudent, and where the ability to outline a duration or "end" of an LLC agreement makes the most business sense.

LLC's vs. C Corporations

When entrepreneurs consider starting a business, or when existing small business owners consider changing their business structure, they are often evaluating between the limited liability companies (LLC) and the C Corporation as the entity type for their business.

While LLCs and C corporations have some similarities, most notably limited liability protection for owners, they also have a number of distinct differences. If you are one of the business owners considering these two structures, this section will help you compare LLCs and C corporations a little more closely.

Similarities

1. Both offer the same limited liability protection for owners, meaning that the owners are

typically not personally responsible for the debts and liabilities of the business.

2. Both are separate legal entities created by a state filing.

3. Both have very few ownership restrictions. The owners are not required to be US residents, and the number of owners is without limitation. Additionally, owners are not required to be individuals (as with S corporations).

4. Ownership (stock with corporations and membership interest with LLCs) can be divided into numerous classes.

The Differences

1. Taxation

• C corporations are separately taxable entities. C corporations file a corporate tax return reporting profits or losses, and any profits are taxed at the corporate level. C corporations face the possibility of double taxation when profits are distributed to shareholders in the form of dividends, as the shareholders must report dividends as personal income and pay tax on them at the individual level.

- LLCs are typically pass-through tax entities. While LLCs do complete a business tax return, the profit or loss of the business is passed-through to the owners' personal tax returns, where it is reported and any necessary tax paid at the individual level.

2. Ongoing Formalities

- C corporations face more

extensive internal formalities, including adopting bylaws, issuing stock, holding initial and then annual meetings of directors and shareholders, and keeping the minutes of these meetings with the corporate records.

• While LLCs are not subject to the same internal formalities, they are encouraged to adopt an operating agreement, issue membership shares, hold and document annual meetings of the managers and/or members, and properly document all major decisions of the company.

3. Transferability of Interest

• A shareholder of a C corporation typically is not required to get approval from the other shareholders before selling stock.

- A member of an LLC typically must receive the approval of the other members before ownership can be sold.

4. Management

- The management of an LLC can be by members, in which case the management is much like that of a partnership. If the management of an LLC is by managers, then the management structure more closely resembles that of a corporation, since the members will not be involved in the daily business decisions of the company.

- C corporations have directors and officers. The board of directors oversees and directs the affairs of the corporation and has responsibility for major decisions, but is not responsible for the day-to-day operations of the corporation. The directors elect officers to manage the daily affairs of the business.

5. A C corporation's existence is perpetual. Conversely, an LLC typically has a limited life span. Most states require that LLCs list a dissolution date in the formation documents (typically called the articles of organization or a certificate of organization), and certain events, such as death or withdrawal of a member, can cause the LLC to dissolve.

LLC's vs. S Corporations

When entrepreneurs consider starting a business, or when existing small business owners consider changing their business structure, they are often evaluating between the limited liability companies (LLC) and the S corporation as the entity type for their business.

While LLCs and S corporations have some similarities, most notably limited liability protection for owners and pass-through taxation, they also have a number of distinct differences. If you are one of the business owners considering these two structures, this section will help you compare LLCs and S corporations a little more closely.

Similarities

1. Both offer the same limited liability protection for owners, meaning that the owners are typically not personally responsible for the debts and liabilities of the business.

2. Both are separate legal entities created by a state filing.

3. Both are typically pass-through tax entities. While both entities file business tax returns, the profit or loss of the business is passed-through to the owners' personal tax returns, where it is reported and any necessary tax paid at the individual level.

4. Both are subject to external formalities, such as filing annual reports, which are required by the state, and paying necessary annual fees.

The Differences

1. Ownership

• The Internal Revenue Service (IRS) restricts ownership of S corporations, while LLCs do not face the same restrictions. Some of the IRS restrictions include:

- LLCs can have an unlimited number of members (owners) while S corporations can have no more than 100 shareholders (owners).
- Non-US residents can be members of LLCs, while S corporations may not have non-US residents as shareholders.
- S corporations cannot be owned by C corporations, other S corporations, LLCs, partnerships, or many trusts. LLCs are not subject to these same restrictions.

2. LLCs are allowed to have subsidiaries without restriction.

3. Ongoing Formalities

- S corporations face more extensive internal formalities, including adopting bylaws, issuing stock, holding initial and then annual meetings of directors and shareholders, and keeping the minutes of these meetings with the corporate records.

- While LLCs are not subject to the same internal formalities, they are encouraged to adopt an operating agreement, issue membership shares, hold and document annual meetings of the managers and/or members, and properly document all major decisions of the company.

4. Management

- The management of an LLC can be by members, in which case the management is much like that of a partnership. If the management of an LLC is by managers, then the management structure more closely resembles that of a corporation, since the members will not be involved in the daily business decisions of the company.

- S corporations have directors and officers. The board of directors oversees and directs the affairs of the corporation and has responsibility for major decisions, but is not responsible for the day-to-day operations of the corporation. The directors elect officers to manage the daily affairs of the business.

5. An S corporation's existence is perpetual. Conversely, an LLC typically has a limited life span. Most states require that LLCs list a dissolution date in the formation documents (typically called the

articles of organization or a certificate of organization), and certain events, such as death or withdrawal of a member, can cause the LLC to dissolve.

6. The stock of an S corporation is freely transferable, as long as IRS ownership restrictions are met. The membership interest (ownership) of an LLC typically is not. Approval of the other members must be received.

7. An S corporation may have advantages with self-employment taxes in comparison to the LLC. For more information on this issue, please contact your accountant or tax advisor.

Information Frequently Required on LLC Formation Documents

The formation document for an LLC is called the articles of organization or certificate of organization. Each state has its own version of this document creating a number of variances in the amount and type of information required.

Company Name: The desired name of the LLC must be included. That name must typically contain an LLC identifier, such as "Limited Liability Company," or an abbreviation, such as "LLC" or "L.L.C." Undertaking a preliminary name availability search prior to submitting the articles of organization will help to see if your desired name is available. Keep in mind that the state holds final approval rights on the desired name to ensure it is not already in use by another company in that state or is not "deceptively similar" to a name already in use.

Business Purpose: The business purpose is an explanation of what the company is formed to do or provide. There are two types of business purpose clauses: general and specific. *General business purpose* – some states will accept a general-purpose clause, which basically states that the company is formed to engage in "all lawful business."

Specific business purpose – some states require a more complete explanation the types of products and/or services the company will provide. Registered Agent: Virtually all states require LLCs to have a registered agent in the state of formation. The registered agent is the party responsible for the receipt of important legal and tax documents for the LLC. The registered agent must have a physical address (no P.O. boxes) in the state of formation and must be available during normal business hours.

Examples of documents sent to the registered agent include Service of Process (or notice of litigation), which is the document that initiates a lawsuit; mail from the state; and often taxation documentation from the state's department of taxation.

One thing to note is the registered agent address is a matter of public record. In states that do not require the legal address of the business to be included in the formation documents, the registered agent address is the only address on file for the company. Many business owners, particularly home-based businesses, choose to use a registered agent provider both to ensure these important documents are professionally handled to keep their addresses out of the hands of marketers.

Organizer: The organizer is the person or company preparing and filing the articles of organization with the state. Most states require the name and signature of the organizer to be included in the formation documents and some also require the organizer's address be included.

Management Structure: LLCs can be managed by members or by managers, and the articles of organization must state which group will manage the company. When an LLC is managed by members (owners), it more closely resembles a partnership. When an LLC is managed by managers, it more closely resembles a corporation since the owners will not be involved in the daily business decisions of the company.

Members or Managers: Many states require the names and addresses of the initial members (if the LLC is member-managed) or managers (if the LLC is manager-managed) are included on the formation documents.

Legal Address of the Company: Supplying the legal address, or the principal address, of the business is optional in many states but a few states do require it.

How to Form an LLC
Do I need two members?

Many states allow for the creation of single-member LLCs. Other states require two or more members. It is important to remember that the IRS may apply different tax liabilities to a LLC with only one member (taxed as a corporation or disregarded entity for tax purposes) than it does to an LLC with more than one member (taxed as a partnership by default).

Must I hold LLC meetings?

In many states, an LLC is not required to hold the simple member/manager meetings in order to maintain the protection provided against liability as are required by officers/directors and shareholders of corporations. For example, California does not require member/manager meetings unless the LLC's Articles of Organization specifically require them

Who votes in an LLC?

In most cases, voting rights are

proportional to the percentage of membership ("ownership") interest. However, the articles of organization or operating agreement may establish a different set of criteria for voting rights

Can I sell Member Shares?

Typically, member shares may be sold only upon the approval of members holding a majority in interest, unless otherwise stipulated by the articles of organization or the operating agreement...

How long does an LLC endure?

Many states now allow an LLC to have a perpetual existence. In the past LLC's were required to provide a date on which the LLC's existence would terminate. In most cases, unless otherwise provided in the articles of organization or a written operating agreement, an LLC is suspended upon death, withdrawal, resignation, or bankruptcy of a member, with some exceptions.

Do I need an Operating Agreement?

Yes, the complete the creation of an LLC includes the drafting of an Operating Agreement. The Operating Agreement must be created, either prior to or directly after the filing of the Article of Organization. An Operating Agreement may be either oral or written.

What paper work is required to form an LLC?

The Articles of Organization must be legally drafted and filed with the state office. Initial fees must also be paid at this time.

What are the advantages of a

LLC?

An LLC is a combination of the best aspects of a partnership and a corporation. LLCs provide liability protection for member/owners (with a few exceptions), establishing a separate entity from the individual member/owners. However, an LLC does not require all the formalities of its managers and members that are required for a corporation. Additionally, many states allow the formation of single-member LLCs.

What are the disadvantages of a LLC?

There is no reliable continuity. If a member is dismissed, dies, is disabled or resigns, the LLC is dissolved unless the Articles of Organization or Operating Agreement state otherwise. When the LLC is formed, some states require that a date for the future dissolution of the LLC be recorded. On the other hand, a corporation would continue to exist as an entity in the event of the death, disability or dismissal of a director(s) or officer(s).

There a great deal of paperwork involved in the creation LLC.

Should I choose an LLC or an S corporation?

This decision depends on your individual business and financial structure and situation. If you have questions regarding this you should contact a financial professional or an attorney. An S corporation avoids the "double taxation" inherent in other business organizations but is not a flexible as a limited liability company. Only WE citizens and WE resident aliens may own an S corporation.

There is a limit of 75 shareholders.

An LLC may offer different levels/classes of membership while an S corporation may only offer one class of stock. There is not a limit to the number of people who can own an LLC. An LLC can be owned by a US or foreign person, a corporation or another LLC. However S corporations cannot be owned by other corporations, most trusts, LLCs, partnerships, or nonresident aliens. Additionally, LLCs have no restrictions on subsidiaries.

How is an LLC taxed?

An LLC can be taxed for federal income tax purposes as a partnership.

An LLC can choose partnership status in order to avoid taxation at the entity level. If an LLC is not taxed as a partnership it is often taxed as a C corporation (as chosen on the IRS 8832 form). Some owners of LLCs elect choose for their LLC to be a "disregarded entity" for taxation purposes where the owner is fully responsible to report the taxes on his or her personal tax returns.

What is the organizational structure of an LLC?

An LLC is owned by its members. The business organization may resemble either a partnership or a corporation depending on who exercises managerial responsibility. An LLC resembles a partnership if managers are not used. In this case the members have a direct say in the managing and day to day activities of the company. An LLC would resemble a corporation if its members choose to use managers to administer to the day to day activities of the company because the members will not typically participate in the day to day management.

LLC Formalities

Limited Liability Companies are becoming more and more popular as an excellent company organizational vehicle for conducting business, with very good reason. They offer untoward flexibility with respect to management and operation, excellent protection from liability, and they offer profound taxation benefits in the form of their pass-through taxation. There almost seems to be a scramble by some states to lure corporations in general, and LLC's in particular, to them in the form of very business-friendly acts and legislative moves. Even so, there are certain operational and organizational steps, sometimes known as "LLC formalities," that must be taken and adhered to in order for the members to enjoy all of the limited liability and taxation benefits afforded the LLC.

Piercing the LLC Veil

"Piercing the corporate veil" is the equitable remedy courts use to disregard the corporate structure, and this can translate into a piercing of the "LLC veil." If a corporation is found not to be operating in observance of the formalities, an owner is exercising excess control, funds are being grossly misappropriated for the benefit of an owner, or if the corporation is deemed to be operated in such a manner as to cause harm to another entity, the courts can pierce the corporate veil and make the owner(s) personally liable for any debts or obligations of the company. The same can be true, although admittedly to a lesser extent, of an LLC. If a member exercises excess control over the entity, if the member in control engages in improper conduct in the exercise of control over the entity; and this improper conduct causes another entity to be denied adequate remedy in a lawsuit or business transaction proceeding, some courts may "pierce the LLC veil" and make the members or managing member directly responsible for the debt or obligation.

Traditionally, courts have looked at numerous factors to determine whether a controlling member/shareholder engaged in improper conduct. Chief among these factors would be the lack of an operating agreement, or a poorly written one. Too, a failure to maintain adequate records of acquisitions, business transactions, and in some states, minutes of meetings could lead a court to disregard the entity and hold the controlling member personally liable. While the rules for observing the corporate formalities are not as stringent for an LLC, there are obviously still some semblances of formalities that must be observed.

Having a well-written operating agreement in place should be obvious by now, but there are a couple others. The important ones (but by no means the only formalities) are listed below.

LLC Formalities

- Having a well written Operating Agreement in place, with well defined roles for members, well outlined distribution guidelines, and operational and taxation rules.
- Adequate records for all transactions and business engagements, as well as properly written minutes of meetings (at least one state, Tennessee, requires an annual meeting of the members). List of members, past and present, articles of organization, tax returns for the past three years, bank statements, resolutions authorizing activities that, either by law or under the terms of the operating agreement, require a vote of the members, etc. Are all examples

of the types of records and written agreements that should be properly maintained by the LLC

• Adequate capitalization for the company and maintaining proper operating capital

These are but a few, though vital, suggestions of formalities that should be observed. Other actions, or lack thereof, that could lead to the piercing of the LLC veil include:

• Actions not covered in the Operating Agreement of an LLC--this is tantamount to disregarding the LLC formalities. Although an LLC is technically not required to observe formalities in the same manner that a corporation is, its actions should be completely guided by the operating agreement, and this agreement is taken into consideration by the courts and tax authorities when a determination is made as to the operation of the LLC.

- Deficient or inadequate capitalization is another important deficiency that a court or tax regulator will examine when determining the intent of the LLC and its member's and will usually factor heavily in their decision to pierce the veil. It is important that an LLC be properly capitalized and funded, and that the members manage the funds properly in order to run business properly. Siphoning too many assets or capital and leaving too little in the coffers to satisfy creditors or company operations may lead to a veil-piercing determination.

- Co-mingling of funds is a bad idea in any form of corporation or LLC. Any sense of co-mingling of funds or accounts will almost certainly lead to an "alter-ego" determination by the courts or a tax regulatory board and will lead once again to veil piercing--thereby risking personal assets and stripping members of the liability and asset protection. It is a best-practices act to make certain that separate accounts are maintained and monitored.
- The amount of discretion shown by the members should be metered to ensure that all actions are deemed to be in the best

interest of the LLC or the business. Personal agenda's should come secondary to the LLC as a whole, lest it be determined that it was formed for an express personal agenda and not a business goal.

- The LLC should never be treated as an extended personal account of its owners or members. The courts and tax regulatory boards regularly examine the financial dealings and workings of an LLC to determine whether it is a working business or an independent profit center for its owners or members. If it is deemed an independent profit center, the veil could be pierced and there can be tax penalties and liabilities against the owner or members personally.

An LLC should pay and guarantee its own debts, unless specifically outlined in the operating agreement for specific requirements for such things as the rental or leasing of real property, etc. At times, if an owner or member regularly guarantees or pays debts, he will have been shown to act as an alter ego of the LLC and hence will cause that LLC to lose its separate entity status. Owners should not pay or guarantee the debts of their own LLC unless it is specifically outlined in the operating agreement for specified purposes.

So while a "formal" set of rules is not a requirement outlined by any state for an LLC, the concerned and astute business man or LLC member will understand that there are LLC formalities to be followed and adhered to in order to fully enjoy the benefits afforded by the LLC.

LLC Management

While the formation and structure of an LLC can be quite rewarding to its members, the proper operation and management of the LLC is not without its perils and requires careful forethought. It is never too early to consider the management style of the LLC and the style and strategic goals should be reflected in the Operating Agreement and the structure of the LLC. As flexible and organizationally moldable as an LLC is, it is imperative that the selection of key management goals is outlined, the empowerment of certain members is delineated, and the income distribution and taxation goals be stated, as soon as is possible. In addition, care must be taken by the Managing Member to ensure that the integrity of the LLC's separate entity status is maintained; thereby safeguarding its tax position and the limited liability protection afforded its members.

Much in the same manner that Corporations can be subject to a piercing of the corporate veil by outside agencies or adverse parties in a lawsuit, the LLC can be bereft of the corporate protection if the LLC status is jeopardized because of mismanagement or misappropriation of its funds or assets. The manner in which to lose this protection is very similar to that which a standard Corporation loses its veil. If, for example, a court of law deems that the members acted in such a way that company funds were treated as their own, or if the LLC was a de-facto shield for tax evasion purposes, or if the corporate form was abused or completely disregarded by the members, then they would be considered to have lost their LLC status and would be subjected to having the LLC veil pierced. In addition, the court can also invoke the doctrine if it feels that the LLC was managed or dominated in such a way that it was wielded in order to inflict an injury, fraud, or an injustice against an outside individual, group, or organization.

It is the Managing Member's prime directive to ensure that none of these things occur at any point during the formation or operation of the LLC.

Although no proper "Corporate Formalities" apply to an LLC, the courts nonetheless expect the LLC to be managed within the parameters of a "corporate form," with some basic premises and understandings. There are very important points that must be considered in order to effectively manage an LLC:

- Executing an Operating Agreement and preserving its integrity. This is the agreement that governs the operation and management of an LLC, and is the closest thing to a Corporate Formality that an LLC experiences. This is the place where all of the distribution, taxation, and goals of an LLC should be clearly outlined so that there is no question of intent as to each of these points. This is also the place where any special privileges to key members are outlined.

• Ensure that there is adequate capitalization for the formation, operation, and maintenance of the LLC. This is another management area that comes under close court scrutiny whenever the LLC status is brought into question. Inadequate capitalization may reek of fraud to the court and may lead to a piercing of the LLC veil. It is the Managing Member's responsibility and directive to ensure that LLC funds are properly managed, and that there is no misuse of funds or excessive or unnecessary depletion of assets by the members. Improper use of funds or leaving not enough operating capital in the coffers is a sure-fire way to attract untoward regulatory or court attention and lead to a piercing of the veil.

- The Managing Member should ensure that there is absolutely no Co-mingling of funds. This means that in no way should any of the LLC funds be used for personal purposes or advantage by members, nor should members be directly responsible for the payment or guarantee of an LLC debt or financial obligation. Any form of personal use of corporate funds or assets will most assuredly lead to an alter-ego interpretation by the court or regulatory agencies which inevitably lead to a loss of LLC status and all the protections afforded by such status.

- All Members should adhere to the principles outlined by the Operating Agreement, and understand that all official actions on behalf of the LLC should be applied against a "in the best interest of the LLC" standard to ensure that there are no personal agendas proffered at the expense of the health of the LLC. Any actions to the contrary can also lead to an alter-ego determination by the court and result once again in the piercing of the LLC veil. Taxation is another area where effective management can lead to successfully taking advantage of all of the tax benefits afforded the members. The avoidance of excessive taxation is one of the important reasons companies choose to incorporate as LLCs, and it is of prime importance that these benefits are safeguarded through an effective Operating Agreement and efficient management. It is in every member's interest that these benefits are preserved through effective and efficient management.

Having a proper management plan, and authoring a thorough and effecting Operating Agreement, will go a long way towards ensuring the prosperity of an LLC, and selecting a like-minded Managing Member is the best place to start.

Improperly Managing an LLC

In order to illustrate how these issues may effectively reduce or eliminate the protection from liability that is afforded by an LLC, let's examine a couple examples:

1. LLC Management Example - Co-mingling Funds

John agrees to invest with Invest LLC, of which Simon is the sole member. Under the investment agreement, Invest LLC establishes an investment profile with 45 days duration, in which John is to recover his investment, plus a 25% bonus. Simon, as the sole member of the Invest, is not properly capitalized. Simon resorts to taking loans on his home in order pay for LLC expenses rather than simply loaning the money to the LLC and issuing a promissory note. He also issues LLC checks for his personal expenses and pays for LLC operating costs from his personal account without reimbursing himself or having a promissory note from the LLC to reimburse himself in the future.

At the end of the duration, John demands his capital investment plus the 25% bonus that was agreed to. Simon is unable to pay the capital and files for bankruptcy protection for his LLC.

In the ensuing court proceedings, John will most likely succeed in piercing the corporate veil and can begin to recover his losses from Simon's personal assets, including his home, investments, back accounts, vehicles, etc.

2. LLC Management Example - Liability Protection

Tony is the only member of Speedy Service LLC, a local package delivery service. Speedy Service LLC's balance sheet shows a net worth of $50,000. Unexpectedly, Better Delivery Corp. opens its doors next to Delivery LLC which causes the market for Speedy Service LLC's services to dwindle. The net worth of Speedy Service drops sharply. Tony is unwilling to add additional capital, and the company soon goes out of business. Jack, who lives in the same city in which Speedy Service LLC does business, is hit by Speedy Service LLC's truck while jogging. Jack brings a suit to pierce the LLC veil of Speedy Service LLC.

Under this scenario, Jack may try to pierce Speedy Service LLC's veil in order to reach Toni's personal assets.

The application of the doctrine to pierce the veil in this manner, whether in the LLC or corporate setting, is considered a drastic remedy by most courts, particularly in instances where the owner is an individual as opposed to another business entity. Accordingly, a court will only in rare circumstances, and after much deliberation, resort to this remedy. It is also important to note that it is perfectly legal to form an LLC to avoid personal liability. Naturally, what will expose the owners is using this financial shelter to engage in criminal activity. Members of an LLC can manage these risks by ensuring that they have a complete and proper management plan in place in the form of a well written and articulate operating agreement. They should ensure that personal business and financial affairs are maintained separate from the LLC, that personal assets and funds be maintained separate from the LLC, and that there is always adequate capitalization in order to ensure the proper operation of the business.

Each member's ownership percentage should be clearly delineated in the operating agreement, along with any enhanced ownership rights or authorities granted to any one owner. Profit and bonus distribution should also be properly outlined in the operating agreement, along with the members' annual draw or salary. If there are non-member employees of the LLC, their duties, rights, and responsibilities should also be a part of the operating agreement and properly listed within.

Chapter 4: Where to Form your Corporation or LLC?

This is a very important question that bears careful consideration of a number of factors. While you are not required to incorporate in the state of your residence, you must consider things such as analyzing costs of incorporating as a foreign corporation in another state, the physical location of your facilities, if any, and a careful review of what advantages incorporating in a state other than your own might provide.

The fees, regulations and corporate governing laws vary from state to state, as do the rights and privileges assigned to shareholders, directors, and boards. Most people choose to incorporate in their state of residence due to simplicity and ease of filing. If your corporation will be a closely held corporation that primarily conducts business in just one state, then local incorporation makes the most sense as costs will usually be less and the paperwork and filing requirements will usually be less as well. However, there are some very real advantages, depending on the type of business you intend to operate and tax situations you wish to take advantage of, when incorporating in other states such as Delaware and Nevada.

When conducting business in any state other than the one in which you or your business is incorporated in, you will be requires to file a "Foreign Qualification" for that particular state, which will increase the fees and paperwork (e.g. your corporation is formed in Delaware but you wish to conduct business in California, California will require a Foreign Qualification)--not a tremendous hurdle, especially if the business volume warrants the added expense, but definitely worthy of consideration. Consider too that a foreign corporation, once qualified to conduct business in another state, is subject to taxes and annual report fees from both the state of incorporation and the qualifying state in most instances. The advantage of incorporating in a state with very low or no corporate income tax is thus not as great as it may in appear in some instances.

Delaware

As you are evaluating where to form your corporation or LLC, you may be considering Delaware. Maybe you've heard that over half of the public companies and Fortune 500 companies are incorporated in Delaware. While this is true, you should closely assess whether Delaware is the appropriate choice for your particular business.

For large businesses, there are a number of reasons why it is advantageous to incorporate in Delaware; however, these reasons may not be as beneficial to smaller businesses.

Common Advantages of Forming in Delaware

- Delaware's business law is one of the most flexible in the country.
- The Court of Chancery focuses solely on business law and uses judges instead of juries.
- For corporations, there is no state corporate income tax for companies that are formed in Delaware but do not transact business there (there is a franchise tax, however).
- The taxation requirements are often favorable to companies with complex capitalization structures and/or a large number

of authorized shares of stock.

- There is no personal income tax in Delaware for non-residents.
- Delaware does not require director or officer names (corporations) or member/manager names (LLC's) to be listed in the formation documents, thereby providing a level of anonymity.
- Shareholders, directors and officers of a corporation or members or managers of an LLC need not be residents of Delaware.
- Shares of stock owned by persons outside Delaware are not subject to Delaware taxes.

Typically the court system is not a primary factor evaluated when choosing where to form a business; however the Delaware court deserves a special mention. The Delaware Court of Chancery is often considered an advantageous venue for shareholder lawsuits. As mentioned above, the Court of Chancery hears only business cases and uses only judges, no juries. For large corporations with thousands or hundreds of thousands of shareholders, this can be beneficial. For small corporations with only a few shareholders, shareholder suits are unlikely. Also, undertaking a case in the Delaware courts may place more of a burden on a small business versus undertaking a case in a court in the company's home state. Therefore the Court of Chancery does not often hold the same advantages for small businesses that it does for large public companies.

Another factor to consider if you are evaluating forming your corporation or LLC in Delaware is whether you will need to foreign qualify your company in another state.

Corporations and LLC's are considered "foreign" in every state other than their state of formation. Foreign qualification registers a company to transact business in a state other than the home state.

Corporations and LLC's formed in Delaware often need to foreign qualify in their home state, since they have a physical location and employees there. If you are considering Delaware as the state of formation, you should include the initial and ongoing costs of formation and also foreign qualification costs in any other state(s) in your evaluation.

Nevada

Nevada is notable for its lack of state corporate income tax and personal income tax--this can be a boon if taxation is a major consideration. It also allows for a greater level of privacy for corporations and their shareholders. As such, Nevada can be particularly favorable for corporations located in California and other Western US states. While any public corporation can benefit from Nevada's flexible statute, Nevada is particularly attractive to privately-held corporations, as its statute's default provisions geared towards favoring management. As is the case with forming a corporation in Delaware, critics of the formation of corporations in Nevada believe that its laws and courts are excessively friendly to corporations.

Benefits of Nevada Corporations:

- Flexibility to a Board of Directors in managing the affairs of a corporation,
- Permitting management to put in place strong protection from hostile takeovers.
- Courts in that state are more focused on the application of corporate law than the courts of

most other states

- Nevada's courts are developing a strong body of case law that serves to give corporations and their counsel guidance on matters of corporate governance.
- Nevada's tax structure is also a large benefit to incorporation in Nevada. Nevada has no franchise tax. It also has no corporate income tax or personal income tax.
- Disputes over the internal affairs of Nevada corporations are filed in the Nevada State District Courts, and can be appealed to the Nevada State Supreme Court.

Forming a corporation in any of the 50 states offers limited liability, privacy, and tax benefits to one degree or another. Forming a Nevada corporation, however, takes these same concepts to a higher level, offering numerous advantages to the businessman or entrepreneur. Those looking for ultra-low state tax, privacy and confidentiality, a business and corporation-friendly environment will find forming a corporation in Nevada at the top of their list. This is primarily because the Nevada legislative and judicial branches of government have proven quite corporate-friendly and savvy. This pro-corporation approach is reflected in the numerous advantages afforded to Nevada corporations. Initially based at least partially on Delaware Corporate law, the Nevada legislators have taken the Nevada Corporate law even further with respect to high privacy and low taxation rights, as evidenced by their extensive corporate privacy and asset protection/limited liability statutes and regulations, and low to non-existent state taxation.

Privacy and Anonymity

Forming a corporation in Nevada practically guarantees privacy to shareholders and privacy to vice presidents and other corporate officers. Shareholders are not a matter of public record in Nevada, and save for an appointed Director and Registered agents; the names of other officers in a Nevada corporation are protected and private under Nevada law. Unlike some other states, Nevada Corporations can hold their annual meetings anywhere, even a foreign country, with a majority sufficing for a quorum vote for any actions. These meetings can be held telephonically, or via various other "modern" means, leaving the door open to tale-conferencing, the internet, etc.

Nevada Corporate law also allows for "nominee" Director and Officer Appointments that can further enhance privacy and confidentiality. A nominee Director or Officer is one that stands in place of the "true" owner or controlling entity of the corporation. Because Nevada requires that the name of the Director (or Directors) of a corporation be a matter of public record, a nominee Director can be in place as the only publicly disclosed officer or representative of the corporation (along with the Registered Agents, of course). Most nominee Directors or officers usually have minimum signor authority within the corporation, with no control of corporate funds or operational control of the corporation, and can be "voted out" at any time by the majority shareholder or controlling interest in the corporation. Again, because of the flexibility of the by-laws allowed by Nevada, almost any rule with respect to the appointment of nominee officers can be addressed in the bylaws. Basically, these nominee Directors or Officers are such in title only, for public view, with the real controlling entity kept confidential!

Low Taxation

This is another area where a Nevada Corporation can truly benefit your bottom line. The individual nominal taxation rate at the Federal level is approximately 28%--and this is not factoring in such things as Social Security tax, and Medicare tax; these would amount to a total federal tax burden of close to 45% for a non-incorporated individual. If you were to form a Nevada Corporation, the first $50,000 in net income would be taxed at the nominal corporate rate of 15%. This is a difference of 30% of your income!

Now, bear in mind that Nevada Corporations pay zero state income tax. Nevada does not charge franchise tax, capital stock tax, stock transfer tax, estate taxes, corporate income taxes, nor does it tax corporate shares. Because there is no state income tax in Nevada, your corporation would only be subject to Federal taxation. Compare this to what state taxes would be in, say, California, and you can begin to get a clear picture of just what these savings can amount to. Other states, such as California, assess substantial state income tax on corporate income, stock transfers, etc. In addition, if you anticipate your California Corporation to have a tax liability of $500 or more, they mandate that you estimate the taxes and make quarterly payments. There are no such requirements in Nevada, because the state tax amount is

ZERO.

You can form Nevada Corporations in conjunction with a well-thought out tax reduction plan, and develop many tax-reduction strategies based on the proper utilization of your Nevada Corporation.

Limited Liability and Statutory Protection

Nevada is among the most sought after states to incorporate in due in large part because it offers excellent asset protection and limited liability protections to its shareholders, officers, and directors. By statue, shareholder liability is expressly limited to the amount invested in the Nevada Corporation. Quoting directly from the statute: (NRS 78.225) "Stockholder's liability: No individual liability except for payment for which shares were authorized to be issued or which was specified in subscription agreement...no stockholder of any corporation formed in this State is individually liable for the debts or liabilities of the corporation." Further, with respect to Directors or Officers of the Corporation, (NRS 78.747) "...No stock holder, director, or officer of a corporation is individually liable for a debt or liability of a corporation, unless the stockholder, director or officer acts as the alter ego of the corporation." It doesn't get any clearer than that. This is the very definition of limited liability. And the protection doesn't end at the statutory level. When it comes to Nevada corporations, the Nevada courts are reluctant to allow any piercing of the corporate veil, save for extreme case of fraud or in cases involving a complete disregard of the corporate formalities.

No IRS Information Sharing

Unlike most other states in the union, Nevada has no information sharing agreement with the IRS and does not provide personal or corporate financial records to the IRS. There is no reciprocal sharing of financial or business data whatsoever. This can also be a huge advantage to you in implementing your tax-reduction strategies!

Stock Flexibility

Stock flexibility is also a huge advantage afforded to Nevada corporations. Corporate obligations for real estate, services, etc., may be handled by the issuance of stock, at a value determined by the Director. Stock can also be exchanged or sold for cash, goods, real estate, etc. Nevada Corporations can issue different series of stock, with different values and rights, though there must uniformity within the series, and these values and rights should be described in the articles of incorporation, or by resolution of the board of directors.

The stock or shares in a Nevada Corporation may even be in the form of "Bearer Shares". Precisely as the name implies, bearer shares literally provide for direct ownership of the stock by whoever is currently holding the shares. This can ease the temporary transition of ownership of the corporation in the event of an emergency (asset search by potential hostile litigants, for example). This is a fantastic privacy and asset protection feature. Imagine that there was an intense asset search by a court or regulatory agency. If you knew the threat was imminent, you could place the bearer shares in a safe "location or custody" where they are not under your control, and then truthfully answer, when questioned, that you do not, at that moment, own or possess shares in a corporation. You could regain possession of the bearer shares at any convenient point thereafter, and you will not have spoken any mistruths.

Bearer shares could also ease the transition of significant shares of the corporation from one place to another, with the utmost privacy as they are not subject to a normal stock certificate ledger and are valuable merely by possession.

Fast, Simple Incorporation

Nevada corporate regulations make it a very quick and simple proposition to form a corporation. After paying the low initial fee (approximately $125 if net value is $75,000 or less), and an annual corporate fee of only $85 (for an annual filing requirement of a list of directors and officers), the requirements are as follow: (NRS 78.30)

One or more persons may establish a corporation by:

- Signing and filing in the Office of the Secretary of State articles of incorporation; and
- Filing a certificate of acceptance of appointment, signed by the Resident Agent of the corporation, in the Office of the Secretary of State.
- The articles of incorporation must [adhere to Nevada statute], and the Secretary of State shall require them to be in the fore prescribed.

- Nevada corporations can even be formed telephonically or via the internet, and all within 24 hours. There is no minimum corporate capitalization requirement (other than the filing fee), and no minimum number of people required to hold the various corporate officer positions--in Nevada, one person can hold all officer positions if they so desire.

Residency Requirements

Nevada Corporate code has no residency requirements. Other than the mandated legal age of 18, a Nevada Corporation owner can live in any other state, or can literally be a foreigner in another country. This is especially helpful to those seeking to conduct business nationally, yet wishing to minimize their state income tax. However, in order to maximize on the tax reduction benefits of a Nevada corporation, the corporation must be a "resident" Corporation and must have a physical presence in Nevada. But don't fret! There are ways to own "resident" Nevada Corporations from a distance--please see our "Nevada Corporate Headquarters Program" for more information on this valuable service.

Nevada Corporate Formalities Requirements

All states require certain actions on the part of the corporation in order for it to maintain its separate legal entity status. These actions, known as the "Corporate Formalities," are the vehicle by which a corporation shields its shareholders from direct liability and provides for many of the tax and business benefits mentioned. Under Nevada corporate law, the formalities are very basic. These formalities can be summarized as follows:

- Establish clear, thorough Corporate bylaws
- Hold Director and Shareholder meetings at least annually
- Maintain accurate Corporate Minutes and Records in a Corporate Minutes book
- Conduct all Corporate Transactions in Writing
- Ensure that there is no co-

mingling of corporate and stockholder funds.

These are the basic formalities that should be observed in order to maintain the corporate status of your company in Nevada. There are, of course, other requirements, such as annual filing of a list of Directors and officers, but these are also very straightforward and basic.

It should be evident that choosing Nevada as the state to incorporate offers substantial advantages not readily found in other, so-called low regulation states. From privacy to ultra-low taxation, Nevada's favorable business laws are hard to beat!

Chapter 5: C.Y.A. – Cover Your Assets

"It requires a great deal of boldness and a great deal of caution to make a great fortune, and when you have it, it requires ten times as much skill to keep it."

- Ralph Waldo Emerson

The highest level of risk falls on those who think they are immune from litigation. They don't plan, they don't prepare and then they are hit with a devastating lawsuit.

Imagine everything you've worked for on the brink of collapse, sleepless nights, endless depositions, and deep pocket lawyers. Win or lose most small businesses do not recover from a lawsuit.

The greatest risk comes from small business owners who fail to utilize the asset protection provided by a properly structured business entity such as a Corporation or Limited Liability Company. As a Sole Proprietor or Partnership, your personal and business assets are on the line.

"I'm just a small business owner, what do I have to lose?"

Sit down and make a list of all your assets....house, cars, retirement, savings, college accounts, equipment and inventory. When you look at the big picture do you really feel like rolling the dice, crossing your fingers and hoping that the next knock on the door isn't a process server?

The decision to implement an asset protection plan really comes down to a lifetime of hard work and what you're willing to pay to keep it.

Avoid vs. Evade – Legally Pay Less Taxes

There are certain tax advantages that are available to corporations that simply are not available to sole proprietorships or simple partnerships. These include the ability to write off medical benefits provided to employees, to write off business and entertainment expenses, tax-favorable pension plans, and more. Further, depending on the type of corporation formed, there can even be "pass through" taxation benefits than can further enhance the viability of the corporation and avoid double-taxation (when profit is taxed at the corporate level as profit, then again at the individual shareholder level as earned income). Better tax treatment means that your corporation is more likely to attract suitable investors and allow more of the net profit to remain in your coffers.

Another tax advantage not to be taken likely is the protection from audits. It is well documented that sole proprietorships, or individuals filing self-employed Schedule "C" tax returns, are more likely to be audited by the IRS. Conversely, the audit rate for corporations is much lower than the self-employed. Shareholders own, and can be employed by, the corporation, thereby eliminating the need to file Schedule C tax returns.

Another great benefit you can enjoy when you Form a Corporation is the wide array of tax deductions and tax-deductible benefits one can provide to oneself and to the other employees of the corporation. Even a one-person Corporation can enjoy tremendous tax-deductible benefits such as health insurance deductions, travel deductions, automobile deductions, client entertainment deductions, recreational facilities, etc. One of the most beneficial deductions is the pension plan or 401K. Money placed in a properly structured pension plan is tax deductible and the funds grow tax-free for retirement. These benefits alone can justify the existence of the corporation, based on costs alone, many times over.

Liability Protection

The modern business corporation is its own legal entity that has legal characteristics, including being able to transfer ownership without changing its own legal status and being able to continue its existence even if shareholders should die or transfer their ownership by selling their shares of stock. Additional benefits of forming a corporation are that the shareholders have limited liability. This means the shareholder is not personally responsible for the corporation's debt, is insulated from judgments against the corporation, and is not personally affected from the criminal actions of the corporation. In some jurisdictions, there is limited liability for the corporate officers and directors from criminal acts of the corporation.

What is liability protection?

Liability protection for a shareholder of a corporation was invented in the 17th century. In our society, our laws for legal liability mean that it is a situation which a person is liable because of a wrongful (civil and criminal) act against another person.

In general this wrong is an act that our society says would be grounds for a lawsuit. A lawsuit could force the person or corporation who committed this act to rectify the wrong, which generally means paying money to the person or entity who was wronged. This wrong can be the harm of another's body, property, legal rights or a duty if a written law was breached. One reason corporate liability protection was started was because investors were reluctant to invest in a business venture. Often this investment meant that risk of personally guaranteeing the entire debt by financing the project put their personal assets at risk.

In business, a corporation is considered to be a person or a separate legal entity. A corporation is guided by a set of statutory laws and its own internal laws (articles of incorporation, bylaws, policies and procedures) which directs its behavior. This area of law is called business law. In business law, given that the corporation was appropriately formed, the corporation can provide limited liability protection for owners, management, and staff who are working within the confines of statutory law and the corporation's articles of incorporation and bylaws. Without this protection, owners, management, and staff could be personally liable, exposing all of their personal assets, for the actions of the corporation as a legal entity. For this reason, many business owners choose to incorporate which means they have a different role within the corporation than they would have if they ran their business as a sole proprietorship. If something happens to a sole proprietorship and it goes bankrupt, all of the unrelated personal assets, such as the personal residence of the sole proprietor are at risk. In a corporation, a shareholder (owner) will only loose the amount they invested in the form of the value of the stock decreasing.

What is corporate liability protection's relationship to managing risk? Corporate liability protection should be part of an overall strategic plan by the board of the corporation, directing its officers and staff to identify and manage the risk to the corporation.

Why is liability protection important?

Liability protection limits the personal risk of financial ruin for the shareholder(s) if the corporation should go bankrupt or from other unfortunate judgments. A business owner who runs a business as a sole proprietorship or partnership has everything at risk.

What are the benefits from liability protection?

By protecting shareholders from personal liability, a corporation as a legal entity, has the flexibility to own assets which it can borrow to secure financing and enter into contracts. In general, the shareholders are not responsible for the debts and taxes of the corporation. If the corporation should get sued, the creditors can only go after the corporation's assets, not the shareholders personal assets. Another benefit in a publicly held corporation is that by limiting shareholder liability it serves a purpose in allowing huge sums of capital to be raised with less risk to the individual investors.

Is corporate liability protection also called the corporate veil?

Yes, liability protection is commonly called the corporate veil. Piercing of this corporate veil is part of business law that describes a legal decision where the shareholders of a corporation are held personally liable for the debts and liabilities of the corporation despite the general principal that the shareholders are immune from lawsuits where the corporation is the only legal entity held liable. This concept only occurs with privately held business entities. It is difficult to pierce the corporate veil for publicly held companies because of its large number of shareholders.

Who is protected by the corporate veil?

The shareholders of the corporation are protected by the corporate veil.

What does the corporate veil

protect from?

The corporate veil protects the shareholder from the corporation's actions where its actions could be judged liable.

What are some of the considerations for a business owner to consider when incorporating?

In many states, one of the risks a member of the board of director has is the issue of paying taxes and the risk that taxes may not be paid in a timely manner potentially. A non-incorporated business owner may be personally liable if taxes are not paid. A business owner may give serious consideration to incorporating when the business is generating enough profits that the tax payable on such profits equals or exceeds the minimum tax payables in the state in which the business in being conducted.

How is the corporate veil initiated?

The corporate veil is initiated when the corporation is formed and its articles of incorporation have a statement that provides liability protection to its shareholders.

How is the corporate veil maintained?

In privately held corporations, often the principal shareholders also are members of the Board of Directors and may be officers of the corporation. The corporate veil of liability protection is maintained with the articles of incorporation that commonly include an indemnification agreement creating an exemption from incurred liabilities for the directors and officers from their actions. Each state has its own requirements, but generally state laws determine what kind of action a board member must take to void this indemnification. As a general rule, if Board of Directors and officers act in good faith, within the scope of their duties, and avoid wrongful acts, they will be protected by this indemnification clause. Board of directors and officers can guard from personal liability by getting the corporation to pay for their legal defense and to reimburse for any damages. This indemnification clause generally authorizes the corporation to purchase insurance, called director and officer (D&O) insurance to meet the requirements of the indemnification clause.

How is the corporate veil lost?

Protection from personal liability can be lost of the shareholder gives a personal guarantee, if the incorporation process was defective, if a shareholder, director, or officer signs a contract or personally accepts revenues without explicitly stating that the individual is signing on behalf of the corporation, or if a shareholder, member of the board of directors, or officer, conducts himself in a manner that state law could determine to be a wrongful act.

What causes the corporate veil to be pierced?

Courts will pierce the corporate veil, putting the corporation's liability protection at risk, under a number of circumstances. Each state has different requirements, but generally the corporate veil can be pierced if the corporate formalities are not followed such as not having an annual meeting, not keeping minutes, not maintaining proper filings with the state, not maintaining its own property, financial books and accounts; if it was undercapitalized; or if it can be proved that the establishment of the corporation was a sham whose intent was to defraud. This means that the owners, directors and officers cannot co-mingle their personal assets with the assets of the corporation; if principals engage in criminal activities and if a court decides to pierce the corporate veil because state or federal laws were broken.

Other factors courts will look at include the issue of individual control and the amount of financial interest, ownership and control the principals maintained over the corporation and if the principals used the corporation to advance their personal interests. If the interests between the corporation and the principals are so united that the interests cannot be separated, courts may decide to pierce the corporate veil allowing the principals to stand personally in the stead of the corporation. In addition, if it is determined that the formation of the corporation was a "sham", established to facilitate a fraud against third parties, courts may pierce the veil, setting aside the corporation, and allow the victims to recover from the personal assets of the principals.

If the corporate veil is pierced, what are the potential issues?

Depending on the circumstances of how the corporate veil was pierced, at a minimum, the issues for the shareholder is that the shareholder could be personally liable for their actions, putting their entire personal assets at risk.

In summary, for most business owners, incorporating a business to protect their personally liability is a powerful tool. The incorporation process has many other benefits for the principals. A certain amount of legal astuteness is important for the principals to understand these benefits and conduct themselves as principals within the corporation that takes advantage of the benefits of incorporation including corporate liability protection.

Corporations offer more protection than sole proprietorships. As a corporation is formed, a separate, legal entity is formed that is recognized as being separate from its owners (known as "shareholders"). Because of this separate entity status, when a corporation is sued, it is used as an entity different from its shareholders and hence any award or decision against a corporation will not go against the shareholders as individuals--these provisions and the manner by which a corporation is treated by the law serve to protect the shareholders and managers from personal liability. These types of protections are, of course, not part of a business operated as a sole proprietorship--if a sole proprietorship is sued, the owner is personally liable for any judgments or decisions against his company, and can hence lose personal assets and property. But these protections are not automatic to a corporation; there are certain steps and procedures, or "corporate formalities," that must be observed in order to help ensure that these protections are in place.

Asset Protection Plan

When a civil lawsuit is filed, it generally comes from one of two directions: Business and personal. If your company is incorporated and issued by another company for business reasons, and loses said lawsuit, the shareholders will not be required to satisfy the debts of the corporation from their own personal assets. This safeguards assets and properties of the individual shareholders, and as such, is more attractive to potential investors. This is the "limited liability" feature of a corporation. If faced with a personal lawsuit, such as a divorce or an automobile accident, for example, the assets held by the corporation are safeguarded from any ensuing lawsuit or settlements against the individual shareholder--another reason why a properly formed corporation is attractive to potential investors.

Let us apply a few Case Studies of realistic examples of where an asset protection plan would have made all the difference:

Employee Car Accident

You own a popular restaurant in the city that also does delivery. One night, there is an order to be delivered on the other side of town which is assigned to one of your new delivery guys, a clean-cut first year college student.

An hour later you learn your company vehicle has been in a bad accident where the driver and passenger of the other car were taken to hospital with critical injuries.

Several hours after the accident, you learn that your driver had marijuana in his system. Your insurance will not cover this type of accident. Who will?

Your personal assets will become part of the lawsuit unless you had an asset protection plan in place that put a protective wall between you and your business.

Bad Business Loan

Three years ago, you had a great idea to start a computer consulting business. You start your business out of your house and everything is going along great. In fact, you decide to rent some office space and some office equipment for the new up and coming business.

Unfortunately, you become ill and can't keep your business going. The rent and office equipment lease haven't been paid in three months. You get served with papers, to recoup the money and to go after your personal assets.

If you had formed a Corporation or an LLC when you started your business, then you would only be liable for the money invested into the business. The creditor couldn't go after you personally, (unless of course you signed a personal guarantee).

Good Intentions

Your company sponsors an annual charity softball tournament to raise money for the local youth center. During the game a player slides into second base and breaks his leg. The next thing you know you're being sued for $100,000 to cover his medical expenses and his pain and suffering.

Bitter Divorce

Ten years ago, you married the man of your dreams. You shared three happy years of marriage before starting a family with two children. Also, during this time you were successful in building your sports equipment business into a successful retail chain.

In year eight, your marriage starts to fall apart. Within a year and a half, after some bitter disputes, you're able to work out custody and visitation rights with the kids. However, your ex-husband has also decided to sue you for three million dollars and alimony. You are not made of money and the business carries a large over-head, what are you going to do?

How are you going to prove that you don't have this kind of money? If a majority of your assets really belong to a Corporation then those are assets which cannot be touched to fulfill a personal obligation.

Do's & Don'ts of your Plan
1. Be Prepared

The best way to avoid liability is to establish an asset protection strategy before you need it. Once you have been served with a lawsuit, it is too late to start considering your asset protection options.

2. Separate Your Assets

If you own several rental properties, it is wise to separate each property into a different entity. In the event that you are sued, only one property can be named in the suit. Many companies do this with equipment or vehicles. They run their main operating business in a corporate structure and hold property and equipment in a limited liability company.

3. Asset Allocation

Make a list of everything you have to lose. You might be surprised to realize you have more than you thought. This list will become invaluable when putting together your asset protection plan. Be sure to include a column for your business assets and your personal assets.

4. General Partnerships Are Dangerous

As with sole proprietorships, general partnerships do not separate your personal assets from those of your business. However, what make these entities even more risky is partners can commit the entire partnership to any legal contract. You become liable for any commitment your partners may make, with or without your consent.

5. Keeping a Low Profile

You know the old saying "I'd rather be rich than famous". When you've worked hard to get where you are in life, it's difficult not to flaunt it, even a little bit. If you are a small business owner, you are already perceived as being wealthy by your neighbors, family and employees. They don't realize how hard you work just to keep the business going. It's important to keep a low profile and to not voluntarily give anybody reason to think you have more than you do. The only way to truly protect your assets is to take away the incentive to be sued.

6. Signing A Personal Guarantee = Losing Your Personal Assets

If you can avoid it, try never to sign a personal guarantee for a loan, lease or contract. Once you have signed a personal guarantee, you have just let someone by-pass your corporate structure to attack your personal assets if something goes wrong. One way to avoid this is by allowing your company to establish its own credit rating score.

7. Insurance Can Lead To a False Sense of Security

Don't make the mistake and think that just because you have insurance you have nothing to worry about. In fact if you have a big insurance policy you could be putting yourself at risk. When an attorney sees that you have a nice big insurance policy they know most insurance companies will settle vs. allowing a lawsuit to go to court. Now that is fine, that is what you paid for, but when you go to renew your policy you can bet you'll be paying for it on the back end, that's if they allow you to renew.

8. There Will Come a Time when

it's too late

Fraudulent Conveyance: If you are named in a lawsuit or think you might be named in a lawsuit, it is too late to transfer your assets to someone else for "safe keeping". This is called fraudulent conveyance and it will allow the courts to attack those assets even after you have transferred ownership to someone else. That is why it is important to put together an asset protection plan while your legal seas are calm.

Chapter 6: Rules of the Game

In order to be the very best at the game, you have to know everything about it, and execute with perfection. Ignorance is not a viable defense for not abiding by corporate operating formalities.

The essential rules of operation for a corporation are known as the "Corporate Formalities," or "Operating Formalities." These rules were designed to ensure that the separate legal entity status afforded a corporation is maintained, and the observance of the rules ensures that the all of the benefits commensurate with the formation of a corporation are not compromised. These formalities should be observed by all officers, members, and directors of a corporation, with specific duties and implementation assigned as appropriate. Failure to observe these formalities can lead to the "piercing of the corporate veil" by outside regulatory, tax, or other agencies. To pierce the corporate veil means that any entity could hold you liable and sue you for your personal possessions (house, boat, savings and 401k). The limited liability protection that a corporation offers is no longer available at that point. Failure to complete ANY one of the following formalities could result in a "piercing of the corporate veil."

Primary Operating Formalities

The Corporation must maintain an accurate account of all meetings by the board or special meetings held by the shareholders. These accounts, or notes, are known as "minutes," and are maintained in the corporate "minutes book." The care and accuracy of the minutes is a direct responsibility of the corporate Secretary. It is important that thorough and accurate minutes are maintained by the Secretary, as these minutes can prove invaluable against attempts to disprove the separate legal entity status of the corporation by regulatory or other agencies.

There shall be no co-mingling of corporate funds. This means that private assets belonging to a director, officer, or shareholder of the corporation should not ever be "mixed" with the company or corporate funds. Co-mingling can occur via such simple acts as paying company invoices directly from a personal checking account, or conversely, paying a personal auto loan from the company check book.

These types of actions serve to undermine the separate legal entity status of a corporation, and can lead to direct personal liability or the loss of personal assets in the event of litigation, tax, or collections proceedings.

The Corporate Board of Directors must meet at least once a year. These meetings are required by all 50 states, and are the formal meeting during which important strategic corporate decisions are undertaken, such as large acquisitions, mergers, strategic transactional or contractual agreements with other entities, etc. In addition, it is usually during these meetings that decisions regarding corporate leadership are made, and where officer positions are affirmed changed, and even a chairman or CEO is appointed. Attendance is a must by all directors, unless written consent of assignment of proxy vote is granted to another member of the board by the absentee member.

All contractual agreements entered into by the corporation, at the corporate level, must be memorialized in writing, with express consent of the Board of Directors. This includes all financially-binding agreements (loans, lines of credit, etc.), acquisitions (real estate, other corporate entities, capital equipment, etc.), and employment (with officers, etc.). Failure to properly engage other entities or potential employees may result in severe tax or fiscal liabilities, and in extreme cases, may jeopardize the separate legal entity status of a corporation if there are implications that an officer or member of the Board was using the corporation or its assets as his alter-ego.

The implementation and structure of these formalities will of course vary with the type of corporation formed, but the basic, essential structure is the same. These formalities are an essential component of the corporate operation and should be adhered to as a matter of course. Failure to adhere to the corporate formalities will often lead to a weakening of the asset protection, and limited liability protection, afforded by the formation of a corporation, with the commensurate consequences.

Corporate Compliance

After you have incorporated, you

must adhere to some basic formalities to ensure maximum protection; specifically, proper organization and maintaining your corporate standing on an annual basis. Typically this only involves a few simple items: Filing an annual statement of information, or report, with your home state of incorporation, and keeping proper annual meeting minutes and corporate records.

These formalities could be the difference between liability protection and having your personal assets exposed. By law, a corporate business entity is a separate legal person. In order to maintain its separate legal status, it must act in accordance with federal, state and local government statutes. This means filing taxes, applying for all local business licenses and maintaining corporate formalities.

Business Licenses: A Necessity for Every Business

A common mistake new business owner's make at the time they are starting their businesses is to not investigate and obtain all the necessary licenses and permits. It is a rare occurrence when a business does not require some form of state or local business license. Learning what types of licenses and permits your particular business requires does not have to be a daunting task, but first you should understand the different types: federal, state and local.

Federal licenses are typically only required for businesses that are regulated by a federal agency. Examples of federal agencies that supervise types of businesses include the Securities and Exchange Commission, which regulates companies providing financial advice, and the Bureau of Alcohol, Tobacco and Firearms. Federal permits are granted by the appropriate agencies.

There are different types of state licenses. There are those necessary for occupations and trades that require a specific amount of certified education and/or training, such as doctors, lawyers, accountants, barbers, real estate agents, etc. Many states have licensing requirements for bars and restaurants. Additionally, most retail businesses will require a sales tax license. State licenses are typically granted by the state agencies regulating your particular type of business or by the state department of taxation.

On the local (city and/or county) level, most businesses will require a general business license, which grants the business the authority to operate in a particular city or county. There are often local tax-related licenses. There are also a plethora of different types of permits, which may be necessary based on the location of your business and the type of business you operate. Permits are those that state you are in compliance with local ordinances that govern things such as the appearance of the community and safety to consumers. Examples of local permits that might be necessary include health department permits (if your business is involved with food preparation), sign permits (that govern the appearance and/or location of the business sign), fire department permits (that govern public safety of your location), etc.

If you plan to operate a home-based business, you will need to check on the zoning requirements. Some cities prohibit certain business activities in residential areas. If this is the case for your location, you may be able to petition the appropriate agency for a variance, which is an exception, allowing your business to be operated from your home. Check with your city or county zoning office on the zoning ordinances for your particular neighborhood and business. There are a few other items, which are not business licenses per se, but are often required or may be beneficial, including:

• A federal tax identification number – This number, which is also called an employer identification number or <u>EIN</u> is basically a social security number for your business. The EIN is obtained from the Internal Revenue Service (IRS), and is required on all federal tax returns you file for your business.

• A state tax identification number - Certain states require businesses to have state tax identification number in addition to the EIN.

- DBA – A doing business as <u>(DBA) filing</u>, which is also sometimes called an assumed name or fictitious name filing, allows a business to operate under a name other than the official name. For sole proprietorships and general partnerships, the name of the business is the same as the owner's name. For example, if John Smith has a consulting business that he operates as a sole proprietorship, the company name is John Smith; however, he could file a DBA to have the business known as Smith's consulting. Corporations, limited liability companies (LLC's) and other state-formed business entities can also file DBAs to transact business using a name other than the name included on their state formation documents.

To learn which business licenses may be necessary for your particular business, you can contact the appropriate state and local agencies to inquire about requirements and application procedures. As a new business owner, you'll want to ensure your business is starting on the right foot by complying with all the laws and ordinances governing your type of business and location.

Annual Meetings

State law and federal requirements, such as SEC rules if the corporation is publicly traded, prescribe the information that must be submitted for a vote of shareholders. State law generally outlines the requirements for the annual meeting for publicly held and privately held corporations, for profit and non-profit corporations. In all 50 states, Corporations are required to hold a meeting of the shareholders on AT LEAST an annual basis.

Annual Meetings for Corporation's Shareholders

At a minimum, often the annual meeting is where the annual report is given to the shareholders; shareholders elect the Board of Directors, and may elect the external audit firm that prepares the financial statements for the annual report.

Often the annual meetings disclose who is on the board auditing, nominating and compensation committees and the board member's independence and expertise to serve on these committees. In essence, the annual meeting is an opportunity for the shareholders to vote on issues important to the corporation.

For publicly-held corporations, US Securities and Exchange Commission has an extensive set of rules governing the annual meeting and disclosures to shareholders prior to the meeting. These rules may include requirements for the annual report that is issued at the annual meeting and prescribes the information of how directors are to be elected, management remuneration issues are agreed upon, management transactions are approved, governance and beneficial ownership is noted, comparative performance of the stock compared to its peers and market indices, and the financial report.

Complicating the annual meeting logistic planning may be the need to obtain proxies from the shareholders so that the quorum requirements can be met and allow shareholders to pass certain resolutions. The proxies may include the type of proxy, directors to be elected, issues to be voted on (including any substantial interest each nominee, director, executive officer or associate may have in the issue), disclosure of conflicts of interest and business relationships, bankruptcies, criminal convictions, securities laws violations and other litigation where director and executive officer nominees may cause problems for the corporation, financial disclosures and loans exceeding prescribed amounts, substantial payments to executive officers, law, and investment banking firms. Proxies may include discretionary authority to vote in the proxy's discretion on other matters that come before the meeting, but not elections for office which a bona fide nominee is not named. The proxy should have a fore/against box to be checked. Generally state law makes a provision for the shareholder signing and dating the proxy. Proxies generally are for only one annual meeting.

Disclosures at the shareholder annual meetings often include the report of the audit committee including financial statement, internal controls, and independence issues were discussed with the independent accountants, if the audit committee has a charter, the number of meetings held and the director's attendance record, information on the independent public accountants, compensations received by directors including board meeting and committee meeting fees. Disclosures may include all compensation for the CEO and four highest paid executive officers. Disclosure may include the price trend of the corporation's stock, comparison with peers and indexes, audited financial statements, description of businesses, identify of current directors and executive officers. Even if a company has a controlling stockholder with sufficient voting power to avoid having to solicit proxies, the SEC information statement rules require that the same information be disclosed to shareholders as would be required to be disclosed in a proxy statement. For accountability and fiduciary responsibility purposes, minutes of the proceedings of the shareholder's annual meeting need to be kept permanently available to stakeholders who are interested in the outcome of the shareholders votes.

Annual Meeting for the Board of Directors

Commonly, after the annual meeting for the shareholders where the Board of Directors is elected for the year, the Board of Directors meets and holds its annual meeting. Generally, state law, articles of incorporation, and the bylaws prescribe the purpose of the annual meeting of the Board of Directors. As a rule the annual meeting is the meeting where the Board of Directors organizes itself and elects its Chairman of the Board and board officers. Generally the board officers include a position, generally called the Vice Chairman or President, who will step into the Chairman's position if the Chairman is unable to perform his duty, a Secretary and Treasurer. Bylaws may require that the Board of Directors elect chairman of committees reporting to the Board of Directors. For accountability, liability, and fiduciary responsibility purposes, minutes of the annual meeting are important and prepared to be kept permanently.

What Other Types of Meetings

The types of meetings are generally described in the corporation's bylaws. The bylaws also will describe how the meetings are called, by whom, how notices are given out announcing the meetings and what constitutes a quorum.

Organizational Meeting

Besides the annual meeting outlined above, the organizational meeting often is the first meeting of the new corporation where it organizes itself with its shareholders and elected a Board of Directors. It may ratify the actions of the incorporator, elect the directors and officers, adopt a resolution to establish a bank account, authorize the board and officers to file required forms with the state and federal authorities, reimburse expenses, and set the date of the shareholders annual meeting and meetings of the Board of Directors. The organizational meeting is important because many state laws require this meeting in order for the incorporation process to be completed with the actual organizational meeting. Many states require that the results of the meeting be filed with the state authority regulating corporations. Therefore minutes of the organizational meeting are important and need to be prepared and permanently retained.

Special Meetings

The bylaws generally describe how special meetings are held and may include how the agenda, notices, quorums are detailed so that the corporation is accountable to its stakeholders and the Board of Directors and executive officers are maintaining their fiduciary responsibilities.

Foreign Qualification

When it is determined that a corporation or LLC is transacting business in a state or states other than its state of formation, the company is required to foreign qualify in those states. The process of foreign qualifying a business notifies a state that a corporation or LLC, which was not formed in that state, is transacting business within its borders.

In order to foreign qualify a corporation or LLC; you must register for a certificate of authority in that state. The process of applying for a certificate of authority is similar to filing articles of incorporation or articles of organization. The appropriate documents must be prepared and filed, and the appropriate state fees paid.

As part of the foreign qualification process, a name availability search must be conducted in the state of qualification. This helps to ensure that the name of your company is not already in use in that state by another domestic or foreign corporation or LLC or that its name is not deceptively similar to another name already in use. If your desired name is not available, your company will be required to use an assumed name in that state.

Once the name availability search has been performed, the certificate of authority should be drafted. Each state has different requirements for the information to be included in this document. Common information includes:

- Company name
- Date and state of incorporation/organization
- Principal or legal address of the business
- Name and address of registered agent in the state of qualification

- Name and addresses of officers (for corporations) or members (for LLCs)
- Number of authorized shares and a listing of the different classifications of stock (for corporations)
- Type of management (for LLCs)
- Signature of a corporate officer, often the president (for corporations), or of a member (for LLCs)

Keep in mind that the registered agent must have a physical address (no P.O. boxes) in the state of qualification, and must be available during normal business hours. In case you don't know exactly what the registered agent is or does, the registered agent is the party responsible for the receipt of important legal and tax documents for the company, such as Service of Process (the document that initiates a lawsuit), mail from the state, and often tax documents from the state's department of taxation.

If you do not have a physical address in the state of qualification, you can enlist the services of a <u>professional registered agent service provider</u>, such as American Corporate Credit Services, which serves as registered agent in all 50 states and Washington D.C. Even if you do have a physical address in that state, you, like many business owners, may still choose to use a registered agent service provider, with one of the key reasons being to ensure these important documents are handled professionally.

Additional information is often required in certain states. Examples of this include:

- Names and addresses of directors (for corporations)
- Duration of the corporation or LLC
- Number of issued shares of stock (for corporations)
- Financial information, including information on assets
- Specific business-purpose clause outlining the type(s) of business the company will undertake

Before granting approval of the certificate of authority, many states want to ensure your company is in "good standing" in the state of formation. In order to do this, they require that a <u>certificate of good standing</u> be submitted along with your certificate of authority. States that do not require a certificate of good standing typically require a <u>certified copy of your articles of incorporation or articles of organization</u> to be included when you file for a certificate of authority. The certificate of good standing is a document that states that your company has met all the necessary requirements for corporations or LLCs imposed by your state of formation. Failing to file your annual statements or failing to pay or being delinquent in paying your annual statement fees and franchise taxes could cause your company to be in bad standing with the state. Being in bad standing will most certainly cause the intended state of qualification not to grant you a certificate of authority.

The prepared certificate of authority, the certificate of good standing or certified copy of your formation documents should be submitted to the appropriate state agency and the necessary state filing fees paid. Turn-around time for receiving state approval for a foreign qualification varies greatly by state, but you should typically allow six to eight weeks. Most states will allow you expedite the filing for an additional charge. This often reduces the turn-around time to two to four weeks.

The term foreign qualification can often be confusing to business owners. The first thing most of us think of when we hear the term "foreign" is something outside the United States; however, in the world of US corporations and limited liability companies (LLCs), the word foreign has a different meaning. Foreign qualifying a company means that you are registering it to transact business in a state other than the state of formation. Corporations and LLCs are considered domestic only in their state of formation. For example, if you formed your LLC in Delaware, it is only domestic in the state of Delaware. If your LLC is transacting business outside the state of Delaware, it would be considered a foreign LLC in those other states. When you foreign qualify a business, you register for a certificate of authority in the state or states where your company will be transacting business, and pay the necessary state fees. By doing this, the state knows that a foreign corporation or LLC is conducting business within its borders.

If you are currently evaluating whether to form your business as a corporation or LLC in a state other than one where you are transacting business, and you may need to foreign qualify in that state, keep in mind that your business will be subject to ongoing reporting requirements, fees and taxes in both your state of formation and state of qualification. If your business is expanding into new states and you need to qualify it as part of this growth, these initial and ongoing fees should be considered a necessary part of doing business.

What is Considered Transacting Business?

There are many factors used to

determine whether a company is transacting business in a state, and therefore needs to foreign qualify. Some of the common criteria evaluated include:

- Whether the company has a physical presence in the state
- Whether the company has employees in the state
- Whether the company accepts orders in the state
- Whether the company has a bank account in the state

This is not a complete list, and different states may have different criteria. To determine whether your business needs to foreign qualify in a particular state, it is best to seek the advice of an attorney.

Consequences of Not Foreign Qualifying

One of the questions you may be asking is, "What if I don't foreign qualifies with a state in which my company is transacting business?" You've read that there are additional costs to this process, since your company will face initial and ongoing fees both from your state of formation and state of qualification. Maybe this seems like an unnecessary burden; however, state laws require foreign corporations and LLCs that are transacting business within their borders to foreign qualify.

The consequences of not foreign qualifying your business outweigh the costs associated with foreign qualifying. One consequence is loss of access to that state's court system. For example, if an employee or customer within a state in which you are transacting business sues your company, you would not be able to defend the lawsuit in that state's courts, because your company is not recognized as a business there. Another consequence of not foreign qualifying is the possibility of facing fines, penalties and back taxes for the period of time in which your company transacted business within a state without being foreign qualified there.

Foreign Qualifying Versus Incorporating in Every State

There is an alternative to foreign qualifying: you can incorporate your business or form your LLC in the other state(s) in which you intend to transact business. The primary difference is that when you incorporate or form your LLC in multiple states, your company becomes domestic in each of those states, thereby creating separate entities.

For corporations, the increase in corporate formalities is the biggest disadvantage of forming separate domestic corporations. Corporate formalities include drafting and maintaining bylaws; issuing stock and recording all stock transfers; holding initial and then annual meetings of directors and shareholders; and keeping minutes of all director and shareholder meetings with the corporate records. LLCs do not face the extensive formalities imposed on corporations.

When you create a separate corporation in each state, each of these corporations will have its own stock, shareholders, directors, and officers. Even if the shareholders, directors and officers are the same people for each corporation, the formalities must be followed for each domestic corporation, thereby greatly increasing the annual record keeping requirements.

When you foreign qualify, there is only one corporation or LLC. For corporations, regardless of the number of states in which a corporation foreign qualifies, it will require only one set of bylaws, stock, shareholders, directors, and officers. Bylaws will need to be adopted only once, and the holding of and record keeping for the initial and annual meetings of directors and shareholders happens only once. The advantage of forming a new corporation or LLC in each state is the separation of liabilities. For example, if one of your companies is forced into bankruptcy in one state, the assets of the companies in the other states typically would not be used to pay the debts of the bankrupt business. If you have foreign qualified your business in each state, only one corporation or LLC exists, so there is no separation of liabilities.

The Registered Agent

Whether you qualify or incorporate your business in each state, you will need to name a registered agent in that state. Virtually all states require corporations and LLCs formed or foreign qualified in their state to have a registered agent there. The registered agent is the party responsible for the receipt of important legal and tax documents for the company. The registered agent must have a physical address (no P.O. boxes) in the state of formation or qualification and must be available during normal business hours.

Examples of documents sent to the registered agent include Service of Process (or notice of litigation), which is the document that initiates a lawsuit; mail from the state; and often taxation documentation from the state's department of taxation.

Corporate Governance

Corporate governance, a set of processes which includes laws and the corporation's policies, determine the way a corporation is managed. Corporate governance is the term which makes a corporation responsible to its stakeholders by managing its goals and objectives to meet the requirements of the stakeholders. Stakeholders for a corporation can include not only its shareholders, Board of Directors, and executive management, but also its employees, customers, lenders, suppliers, regulators, and the community that it serves. Corporate governance generally means that the corporation must deal with the accountability issues including its fiduciary duty to its stakeholders when implementing its policies and procedures under the direction of laws, regulations, its own articles of incorporation, and bylaws. The purpose of laws and the corporation's own articles of incorporation and bylaws is to ensure the corporation acts responsibly to protect its stakeholders. Because of recent corporate scandals, corporations have been more mindful of corporate governance issues. US Securities and Exchange Commission has a complex set of regulations for publicly traded corporations require ongoing compliance for corporate governance. The last couples of years, Sarbanes-Oxley regulations directly affect larger publicly traded companies but increasingly have an indirect affect of the smallest corporation. As a consequence, corporations increasingly are using the services of external providers to help it meet the many corporate governance issues it faces, including the conduct of the important annual meeting for both the shareholders and the Board of

Directors.

Why is an annual meeting important for corporate governance purposes?

In corporate law a doctrine, the internal affairs doctrine, says that the internal affairs of a corporation will be governed by the corporate statutes and case law of the state in which the corporation is incorporated. Each state's statutes and case law prescribes different remedies and actions for all kinds of the corporation's activities including voting rights, distributions and the obligations of management. The external affairs of a corporation, such as employment and tax liability issues, are governed by the state and federal laws. Other issues governed by state and federal law may include:

contracts, mergers and acquisitions between the corporation and other entities and sales of its securities to third parties. In addition, the internal affairs doctrine for each state requires that a corporation adopt a set of bylaws that govern its actions. These bylaws are the document that drives the actions of the Board of Directors who are responsible for setting the strategic direction of the corporation and hiring management to manage the corporation. One issue the bylaws usually mandate, based on state law, is an annual meeting of the shareholders, where certain issues are presented to the shareholders.

Dissolving Your Business

Unfortunately, for many small business owners, the time comes when they must cease operations and dissolve their business. This is often a very stressful time, and the number of steps involved in dissolving a business doesn't make the process any easier. This page outlines the common steps in dissolving a corporation, limited liability company (LLC), or nonprofit corporation. This information is meant as general information only. It should not be used as a substitute for legal advice. Please seek the services of an attorney, accountant, and/or tax advisor to assist you with the dissolution of your business.

There are six primary steps involved when dissolving a company:

- Corporate action
- Filing articles of dissolution with the state
- Filing all necessary federal, state,

and local tax forms
- Statutory notification to creditors
- Settling creditors' claims
- Distribution of remaining business assets

Corporate Action

The owners of the company must approve the dissolution of the business. With corporations, the shareholders must approve this action. With LLCs, the members must grant approval. For small businesses, the shareholders or members are often involved in the day-to-day operations of the business, and therefore know the circumstances leading to the dissolution.

The bylaws of a corporation and the operating agreement of an LLC typically outline the process for dissolution in terms of necessary approvals. To comply with the formalities of a corporation, the board of directors should draft and approve the resolution to dissolve the company. The shareholders should then vote on that resolution once approved by the directors. Both actions should be documented and placed in the corporate record book. While LLCs are not subject to the same formalities, formally documenting the decision to dissolve the LLC and the members' approval is recommended.

Filing the Certificate of Dissolution with the State

After the shareholders or members have voted to dissolve the corporation or LLC, the appropriate paperwork must be filed with the state in which the business was formed. If the business has qualified to transact business in other states, the appropriate paperwork must also be filed in those states.

The process for filing the certificate of dissolution varies by state. Some states require the documents be filed before notifying creditors and resolving claims. Other states require the documents be filed after that process. To learn more about your state's requirements, contact your Secretary of State's office.

Certain states require tax clearance for the company before the certificate of dissolution can be filed. In these cases, any back-taxes owed by the corporation or LLC must first be paid.

Appendix A - Business Startup Checklist

The checklist below is meant to help new business owners by providing a list of the most common startup steps. Depending on your particular industry, additional steps may be required for your business.

- Prepare a business plan, if you have not done so already. <u>Business plans</u> define the Who, What, When, Where, and How of your business and the products and/or services you plan to provide. Business plans clearly outline the goals of the business, explain the operating procedures, detail the competition, include a marketing plan, and explain the company's current and desired funding. If your company plans to seek funding either in the form of a traditional loan or from venture capitalists, a thorough business plan will be required for the application process.

- Incorporate your business or form your LLC with the state. Forming a business as a <u>corporation</u> or <u>LLC</u> helps to protect the owners' personal assets from the debts and liabilities of the business. There are also other advantages of forming a corporation or LLC, including certain tax advantages and establishing credibility for your new business with potential customers, vendor, employees, and partners. When forming a business, use a professional such as a lawyer or online service like ezcreditservices.com who have experience creating legal entities.

- Select an accountant and attorney. Many small business owners turn to accountants and attorneys for advice when starting out, as well as through the life of the business. Many people seek referrals from friends, family members, or other small business owners in order to find an attorney and/or accountant. You may want to search for professionals who have worked with other small business owners, possibly in your same industry, and are familiar with the unique business situations small business owners often face.

• Obtain the federal tax identification number (also called employer identification number or EIN) for your business from the Internal Revenue Service (IRS). The <u>EIN</u> is like a social security number for a business, and is required for corporations and LLC's that will have employees. The IRS uses this number to identify your business for all taxation matters.

• Obtain the state tax identification number for your business (if applicable). Some states require businesses to also have a state tax identification number. To learn if your state has this requirement, contact your state's taxation department.

- Open a business bank account. It is very important for corporations and LLC's to keep the finances of the business separate from those of the owners. To open a business bank account, most banks require information on the company, such as its formation date and type of business, and names and addresses of its owners. Some banks require corporations to provide a resolution from the board of directors or LLC members/managers authorizing the opening of the business bank account. In New York, a corporate or LLC seal is often required. It is advisable to contact the bank about their business bank account requirements prior to trying to open an account. That way, you will come prepared with all the necessary items.

- Apply for business loans (if applicable). Not all small business owners have enough of their own capital to start a business, and many seek outside funding from sources such as banks or through Small Business Administration (SBA) loan programs.
- Obtain the necessary business licenses and/or permits. Most businesses need licenses in order to begin operations. Licenses may be required for your city, your municipality, your county and/or your state. It is best to contact both your Secretary of State to check on business license

requirements for your particular type of business and industry, and also to contact your local government agency in charge of licensing to learn their requirements and how to obtain the necessary licenses.

- Obtain business insurance. Just as you have personal insurance you should obtain insurance for your business. Some industries may have specific insurance requirements. Discuss your particular industry and business needs with your insurance agent, to ensure you obtain the appropriate type and amount of insurance.
- Investigate other insurance and government requirements. Businesses face a number

government and insurance requirements, particularly if the business has employees. You should investigate your business's obligations for the following:

- ○ Unemployment insurance
- ○ Workers' compensation
- ○ OSHA requirements
- ○ Federal tax
- ○ State and local tax
- ○ Self-employment tax
- ○ Payroll tax requirements (such as FICA, federal unemployment tax, and state unemployment tax)
- ○ Sales and use tax

- Check zoning requirements. This is particularly important if you are starting a home-based business. You'll want to ensure you are meeting your city's zoning requirements for your area.

- Lease office space. If you are not going to be operating a home-based business, you'll probably need to find office space for your new company. Along with leasing an office, don't forget to purchase or lease the furniture and office equipment you will need to get your business up and running.
- Set up your business accounting. You may decide that your accountant will handle the accounting for your business, or you may want to handle the accounting yourself with a small business accounting solution.

Either way, you'll want to ensure that you are prepared to properly account for all business disbursements, payments received, invoices, accounts receivable/accounts payable, etc.

- Establish a line of credit for your business. Establishing a line of credit will help lessen the number of times your new business will be required to prepay for the products and services it purchases. It also helps establish a favorable credit history, which is helpful as your business begins establishing vendor and supplier relationships. As a subset of this, obtaining a D&B D.U.N.S. number for your business is also advisable. D&B (formerly Dun & Bradstreet) is the resource most often used to check the creditworthiness of a business.

- Create business materials. Having materials such as a logo for your business, business cards, and stationery will help your business develop an identity and potential customers find you.
- Develop a marketing plan for your products/services. A primary reason you are starting your own business may be the hope of making money. In order to make sales, people need to be aware of what you're selling and how to find you.

Appendix B – Comparison Chart of Corporation Types

Characteristics	**C Corporation**	**S Corporation**	**Limited Liability Company**
Formation	State filing required.	State filing required.	State filing required.
Duration of Existence	Perpetual	Perpetual	Dependent on the requirements imposed by the state of formation.
Liability	Shareholders are typically not responsible for the debts of the corporation.	Shareholders are typically not responsible for the debts of the corporation.	Members are not typically liable for the debts of the LLC.
Operational Requirements	Board of directors, annual meetings and annual reporting required.	Board of directors, annual meetings and annual reporting required.	Some formal requirements but less formal than corporations.
Management	Managed by the directors, who are elected by the shareholders.	Managed by the directors, who are elected by the shareholders.	Members have an operating agreement that outlines management.
Taxation	Taxed at the entity level. If dividends are distributed to shareholders, dividends are also taxed at the individual level.	No tax at the entity level. Income/loss is passed through to the shareholders.	If properly structured there is no tax at the entity level. Income/loss is passed through to members.
Pass Through Income/Loss	No	Yes	Yes
Double Taxation	Yes, if income is distributed to shareholders in the form of dividends.	No	No
Cost of Creation	State filing fee required.	State filing fee required.	State filing fee required.
Raising Capital	Shares of stock are sold to raise capital.	Shares of stock are sold to raise capital.	Possible to sell interests, though subject to operating agreement restrictions.
Transferability of Interest	Shares of stock are easily transferred.	Yes, but must observe IRS regulations on who can own stock.	Possibly, depending on restrictions outlined in the operating agreement.

Appendix C – Glossary of Terms

- A -

Accrual Method

An accounting method under which income is subject to tax after all events have occurred which fix the right to receive such income and deductions are allowed when all the events have occurred to fix the obligation to pay the debt.

Aggregate Par Value

Aggregate par value is the par value multiplied by the number of authorized shares. This amount is important in determining initial fees and annual franchise taxes in many states.

Annual Meeting of Shareholders

Nearly all states require a corporation to hold an annual meeting of shareholders at which time directors are elected and other corporate issues are voted on.

Annual Report
a required annual filing in a state, usually requiring names of the directors (for corporations), members (for LLCs) and financial information. This term can also refer to an annual statement of business and affairs furnished by a corporation to its shareholders.

Apostle
is a method of certifying a document for use in another country pursuant to the 1961 Hague Convention. With this certification by apostle, a document is entitled to recognition in the country of intended use, and no

additional certification or legalization by the embassy or consulate of the foreign country where the document is to be used is required. An apostillized copy of the articles of incorporation or articles of organization is often required to open a bank account in another country for a US-incorporated business. Note, certain countries require a certified copy of the articles of incorporation/organization with an appropriate gold seal instead of an apostillized copy.

Articles of Incorporation (Certificate of Incorporation or charter). The articles are the primary legal document of a corporation; they serve as a corporation's constitution. The articles are filed with the state government to begin corporate existence. The articles contain basic information on the corporation as required by state law.

Articles of Organization

LLCs must file the articles with the proper state authorities to begin existence. The articles of organization are very similar to a corporation's articles of incorporation.

Asset

anything having commercial or exchange value that is owned by a business, government, institution, or individual. This can include stocks, bonds, real estate, equipment, a brand name, or the value of a company as an operating business, sometimes known as goodwill.

Assumed Name
a name under which a corporation conducts business that is not the legal name of the corporation as shown in its articles of incorporation. Assumed names (also called a fictitious name and Doing Business As or DBA) could be filed at the city, county or state level depending on state requirements. A corporation can use multiple assumed names.

Authorized Shares or Stock
the total number of shares a corporation is authorized to issue. This number is specified in the articles of incorporation. All of the shares authorized need not be issued to shareholders; the corporation can have unissued shares that can

distribute at a later time.

- B -

Board of Directors

the governing body of a corporation. Elected by shareholders, the directors are responsible for selecting the officers and their supervisory roles, and the general control of the corporation.

Business Entity

An organization that possesses a separate existence for tax purposes. Some types of business entities include corporations and limited liability companies.

Business Licenses

There are essentially two types of business licenses, general and special. A general business license, similar to a use tax, is assessed annually for the privilege of operating a business in the jurisdiction. A special license is one that is issued to a business that will provide products or services that require regulation. Special licenses are issued to professionals, such as doctors, lawyers, barbers, and others who have met a certain level of training or education.

Business Permits

State and local governments regulate the safety, structure, and appearance of the community through the use of local laws, called ordinances. Zoning ordinances, which regulate how property can be use, are a common type of ordinance. Once the jurisdiction determines that you have complied with such ordinances, it will issue a permit that will enable you to operate your business.

Business Plan

a written document that details a proposed or existing venture. It will typically explain the vision, current status, expected needs, defined markets, and projected results of the business.

Bylaws

Bylaws are the rules and regulations adopted by a corporation for its internal governance. It usually contains provisions relating to shareholders, directors, officers and general corporate business. The bylaws are adopted at the corporation's initial meeting.

- C -

Capital Gains or Losses

Gains or losses realized from the sale or exchange of capital assets. The amount is determined by calculating the difference between an asset's purchase and sale price.

Capital Stock

See Authorized stock.

Cash Method

an accounting method under which income is subject to tax when actually received and deductions are allowed when actually paid.

C Corporation

A C Corporation is simply a standard business corporation. It is called a C corporation because it is taxed under subsection C of the IRS code.

Certificate of Authority or Application for Authority

Is a document issued by the proper state authority to a foreign corporation granting the corporation the right to do business in that state upon filing an application of authority.

Certificate of Good Standing

A certificate issued by a state official as conclusive evidence that a corporation or LLC is in existence or authorized to transact business in the state. The certificate generally sets forth the corporation's or LLC's name; that it is duly incorporated or organized and authorized to transact business; that all fees, taxes and penalties owed the state have been paid; that its most recent annual report has been filed; and, that articles of dissolution have not been filed. Also known as a certificate of existence or certificate of authorization.

Common Stock

The primary stock of a corporation. This stock gives shareholders the right to participate in management of the corporation and give the shareholder a proportionate share of the dividends.

Conversion

The process of converting a corporation to an LLC or converting an LLC to a corporation. Not all states allow this procedure, and the fees vary within the states that do.

Corporate Kit

A binder usually containing essential items for the routine maintenance and administration of a corporation. Corporate kits include sample minutes, resolutions and bylaws, stock certificates, a corporate seal, and stock ledger.

Corporate Record Book

maintaining the proper records is very important to assure limited liability to corporate shareholders. The corporation should have a record book which contains a copy of the articles of incorporation, bylaws, initial and subsequent minutes of directors and shareholders' meetings and a stock register.

Corporate Seal
a device made to either emboss or imprint certain company information onto documents. This information usually includes the company's name and date and state of formation. Corporate seals are often required when opening corporate bank accounts, distributing stock or conducting other corporate business.

- D -

Delayed Effective Date
Certain states allow for a business to choose an effective date for when the business will officially be formed as a corporation or LLC in that state. For instance, a business owner submitting a formation order in November of 2004 can choose an effective date of

January 1, 2005, when his company will be officially recognized as a corporation or LLC in that state.

Directors

Directors are elected by the shareholders. They manage or direct the affairs of a corporation. Typically, the directors make only major business decisions and monitor the activities of the officers.

Dissolution

The termination of a corporation's legal existence. Dissolution may be caused in many ways including, failure to file annual reports, failure to pay certain taxes, bankruptcy, or voluntary dissolution of the corporation by the shareholders and directors.

Dividend

A dividend is a distribution of money or property paid by the corporation out of the corporation's profits to shareholders. Dividend payments are subject to double taxation, the corporation pays tax on its profits and the dividend recipient must pay income taxes on the dividend payment, the same money is taxed twice. The directors of the corporation decide if a dividend payment is to be made.

Doing Business as (DBA)

A "DBA", also known as an "assumed name", is typically completed by making a filing at the county level where the business is located. This filing does not change the official name of the corporation; however, it allows the company to use additional names.

Domestic Corporation

A corporation is a domestic corporation in the state where it has incorporated.

Double Taxation

Corporations are treated as a separate legal taxable entity for income tax purposes. Therefore, corporations pay tax on their earnings. If corporate earnings are distributed to shareholders in the form of dividends, the corporation does not receive the reasonable business expense deduction, and dividend income is taxed as regular income to the shareholders. Thus, to the extent that earnings are distributed to shareholders as dividends, there is a double tax on earnings at the corporate and shareholder level. S corporations and LLCs are pass-through entities which are not subject to the double tax.

- E -

Equity
The ownership of a shareholder in a corporation.
Escrow
an account set up by a lender to which the borrower makes monthly payments for such obligations as real estate taxes, homeowners insurance, and private mortgage insurance. The lender disburses these funds on behalf of the borrower as the bills become due.

- F -

Fictitious Name
See "Doing Business As".

Fiscal Year
Any twelve-month period used by a business as its fiscal accounting period.

Federal Tax Identification Number
This is a number assigned to a corporation or other business entity by the federal government for tax purposes. Banks generally require a tax identification number to open bank accounts. The federal tax identification number is also known as the Employer Identification Number (EIN).

Foreign Corporation

a corporation is referred to as a foreign corporation in all states except for the state where it is incorporated. If a corporation is "transacting business" in a state other than where it is incorporated, it must register for a certificate of authority to transact business in the other state or possibly lose access to that state's courts and face fines.

Franchise Tax

Is a tax on the privilege of carrying on business as a corporation or LLC in a state. The value of the franchise tax may be measured by amount of earnings, total value of capital or stock, or by amount of business done. In some states, like California, the franchise tax is simply an income tax.

- H -

Holding Company

A corporation that owns a large number of shares in other companies. Holding companies use the voting rights that come with their shares to exert influence over the companies under them.

- I -

Incorporation

The act of creating or organizing a corporation under the laws of a specific jurisdiction.

Incorporator

The person or entity that prepares

files and signs the articles of incorporation.

Involuntary Dissolution
The termination of a corporation's legal existence pursuant to an administrative or judicial proceeding; dissolution forced upon a corporation rather than decided upon by the corporation.

IRS Form 1023
this form is used to apply for tax-exempt status with the IRS.

IRS Form 1120
this form is used to report the income, gains, losses, deductions, credits, and to figure the income tax liability of a corporation.

IRS Form 1120S

This form is used to report the income, deductions, gains, losses, etc. of a domestic corporation that has elected to be an S Corporation by filing Form 2553, and whose election is in effect for the tax year.

IRS Form 2553

this form is used to apply for S corporation status.

IRS Form 8822

this form is used to change your address on file with the IRS.

IRS Form SS-4

This form is used to apply for a federal tax ID number.

- J -

Judicial Dissolution
Involuntary dissolution of a
corporation by a court at the request
of the state's Attorney General's
office, a shareholder or a creditor.

- L -

Limited Liability Company (LLC)
a business entity formed upon filing
articles of organization with the
proper state authorities and paying all
fees. LLCs provide the limited
liability to their members, and are
taxed like a partnership, preventing
double taxation. LLCs can be formed
in every state.

LLC Kit
A binder usually containing essential

items for the routine maintenance and administration of a limited liability company. LLC kits include membership certificates, an LLC seal and sample operating agreements.

LLC Seal

a device made to either emboss or imprint certain company information onto documents. This information usually includes the company's name and date and state of formation. LLC seals may be required when opening bank accounts, distributing membership certificates or conducting other company business.

- M -

Manager

an LLC may be operated by a group

of managers who act much like a board of directors. If an LLC is to Controlled by managers this fact must be stated in the articles of organization.

Member

a member is a person or entity who is an owner of some or all of a LLC. The business decisions of an LLC are made by the members unless the articles of organization provide that the LLC will control by a manager or managers.

Membership Interest

a member's ownership of an LLC is represented by "interests" just as a partner has an interest in a partnership and shareholders own stock in a corporation.

Merger

A merger occurs when two corporations join together into one, with one corporation surviving and the other corporation disappearing. The assets and liabilities of the disappearing entity are absorbed into the surviving entity.

Minutes

a written record which details the events of the corporation. These records should be kept in the corporation's or LLC's record book.

- N -

Name Reservation

The name of a corporation or LLC must be distinguishable on the records of the state government. If the name is not unique, the state will reject the articles of incorporation or articles of organization (for LLCs). A name can be reserved, usually for 120 days, by applying with the proper state authorities and paying a fee.

No-Par-Value Stock

Stock with no minimum value. Most states allow no-par stock. If the stock is no-par stock then the amount of stated capital is typically an arbitrary amount assigned by the board of directors. Some states, though, assign a value of $1.00 to stock when filed as being no-par-value stock. Further, the value of capital for franchise tax purposes is determined by the state and this may result in higher franchise taxes in comparison with low par-value stock.

Not for Profit (or Nonprofit) Corporation

A corporation organized for some charitable, civil or other social purpose which does not entail the generation of profits for shareholders. These corporations can apply for tax-exempt status at both the federal and state level. Not-for-profit corporations, also often called nonprofit corporations, must file not-for-profit articles of incorporation with the state.

- O -

Officers

The directors appoint officers. They manage the daily affairs of the corporation. A corporation's officers usually consist of a president, vice-president, treasurer, and secretary. In most states, one person can hold all of these posts.

Operating Agreement
An agreement among the LLC's members which govern the LLC's operations and the rights of its members. It is analogous to corporate bylaws.

Organizational Meeting
The initial meeting where the formation of the corporation is completed. At the organizational meeting a number of initial tasks are completed such as: the articles of incorporation are ratified, the initial shares are issued, officers are elected,

bylaws approved, and a resolution authorizing the opening of bank accounts is passed.

Organizer

The person who or the entity that prepares, files and signs the articles of organization.

- P -

Paid in Capital

A few states require corporations to have a specified amount of paid in capital prior to starting business. Broadly defined it is all the money and other property belonging to a corporation.

Parent Corporation

A corporation that owns a controlling

interest in another corporation.

Partnership

A partnership is an association of two or more persons. In contrast to a corporation, a general partnership can come into existence without the need to file any formal papers with any state official. The owners of a partnership are personally and fully liable for all business debts; thus, personal property could be taken to pay business debts.

Par-Value

The stated minimum value of a share of stock.

Pass-Through Taxation

The income to the entity is not taxed at the entity level; however, the entity does complete a tax return. The income or loss as shown on this return is "passed through" the business entity to the individual shareholders or interest holders, and is reported on their individual tax returns. S corporations and LLCs are both pass-through tax entities.

Preferred Shares
a class of shares that entitles the holders to preferences over the holders of common shares, usually with regard to dividends and distributions of assets upon dissolution or liquidation.

Professional Corporation
A corporation which is organized for the purpose of engaging in a learned profession such as law, medicine or

architecture. Professional Corporations must file articles of incorporation with the state which meet the state's requirements for professional corporations.

Proxy

if a shareholder cannot attend a meeting, the shareholder is allowed to vote by proxy.

- Q -

Quorum

The minimum attendance required to conduct business at a shareholder or board of directors meeting. Usually, a quorum is achieved if a majority of directors are present (for directors meetings) or outstanding shares are represented (for shareholder meetings).

- R -

Registered Agent

the agent named in the articles of incorporation. The agent will receive service of process on the corporation and other important documents. The agent must be named in the articles of incorporation, and must be located in the state of incorporation or organization.

Registered Office

the office named in the articles of incorporation. The registered office must be where the registered agent is located, and need not be the principal office or place of business of the corporation.

Reinstatement
Returning a corporation or LLC that has been administratively dissolved or had its certificate of authority revoked, to good standing with the state of formation or qualification.

Resolution
A resolution is a formal decision of the corporation, which has been adopted by either the shareholders or the board of directors.

- S -

S Corporation
A corporation which elects subchapter S tax treatment. This tax treatment allows the corporation to avoid entity level taxation.

Section 1244 Stock

An individual investor in a corporation which meets the Section 1244 requirements is entitled to treat up to $50,000 (or $100,000 if filing a joint return) of losses on the 1244 section stock as ordinary losses.

Share

an interest in a corporation. The total ownership of a corporation is divided into shares of stock.

Shareholder

any holder of one or more shares in a corporation. A shareholder usually has evidence that they are a shareholder; this evidence is represented by a stock certificate.

Sole Proprietorship

a business carried on by the owner as an individual. The owner of a sole proprietorship is personally and fully liable for all business debts; thus, personal property could be taken to pay business debts.

Stated Capital

the par value of shares multiplied by the number of shares outstanding.

Stock

an equity or ownership interest in a corporation, measured in shares. Ownership of shares is demonstrated by stock certificates.

Stock Certificate

a written instrument that shows ownership of shares in a corporation.

Stockholder
See shareholder.

Stock Transfer Book
A record book, also called a stock transfer ledger, which lists the owners of shares of stock in a corporation.

Subsidiary
A corporation that is either wholly owned or controlled through ownership of a majority of its voting shares, by another corporation or business entity.

- T -

Tax-exempt Organization
Any organization that is determined by the IRS to be exempt from federal

taxation of income. This determination is based off of IRS acceptance of Form 1023. A tax-exempt organization may be required to operate exclusively for charitable, religious, literary, educational or similar types of purposes.

Treasury Shares
Shares of stock which were issued and later acquired or bought back by the corporation.

- U -

Underwriter
A company that purchases shares of a corporation and arranges for sale of the shares to the general public.

- V -

Voluntary Dissolution

Action taken by shareholders, incorporators or initial directors to dissolve a corporation. Or action taken by members or organizers to dissolve an LLC. The process is completed by filing Articles of Dissolution with the Secretary of State.

Voting Rights

the rights of shareholders to vote their shares pursuant to provisions of state statutes, the articles of incorporation, and the bylaws.

- W -

Withdrawal

The statutory procedure whereby a

foreign corporation or foreign LLC obtains his consent of a state to terminate its authority to transact business there.

ABOUT THE AUTHOR

Robert K Boscarato is an Independent self Published Author who writes about serial killers who have personally affected my life and Historic presidential Assassinations and the business of Business credit